Buddhism:

Discover Ancient Strategies For Beginners or Advanced To Achieve Lasting Happiness, Mindfulness & Calm Stress In The Modern World

Harini Anand

© **Copyright Harini Anand 2019 - All rights reserved.**

The contents of this book may not be reproduced, duplicated or transmitted without direct written permission from the author.

Under no circumstances will any legal responsibility or blame be held against the publisher for any reparation, damages, or monetary loss due to the information herein, either directly or indirectly.

Legal Notice:

This book is copyright protected. This is only for personal use. You cannot amend, distribute, sell, use, quote or paraphrase any part or the content within this book without the consent of the author.

Disclaimer Notice:

Please note the information contained within this document is for educational and entertainment purposes only. Every attempt has been made to provide accurate, up to date and reliable complete information. No warranties of any kind are expressed or implied. Readers acknowledge that the author is not engaging in the rendering of legal, financial, medical or professional advice. The content of this book has been derived from various sources. Please consult a licensed professional before attempting any techniques outlined in this book.

By reading this document, the reader agrees that under no circumstances is the author responsible for any losses, direct or indirect, which are incurred as a result of the use of information contained within this document, including, but not limited to, ─errors, omissions, or inaccuracies.

Gratitude, Joy, Inspiration & Love,

Healing, motivation, inspiration, challenge and guidance straight to your inbox every week....

FIND OUT MORE

Table of Contents

Introduction

Chapter One: An Overview of Buddhism

Chapter Two: The Schools of Buddhism

Chapter Three: Buddhism- Other Concepts

Chapter Four: Buddhism - Ancient Techniques in the Modern World

Chapter Five: Meditation, Yoga, and Buddhism

Chapter Six: Daily Life and Buddhism

Chapter Seven: Buddhism and Karma

Chapter Eight: Buddhism for Kids

References

Introduction

We live in a world that is full of competition, suffering, and pain. Everyone wants to become successful and great. Thanks to the competitive nature of modern society, no one can sit down for a while and relax. Everyone is afraid that if they relax, they will be thrown out of this competition. The human body is a marvel of nature, but it is not made for continuous use. Our body and mind need time to reset and relax.

One of the major problems of this competitive modern world is stress. It is impossible to find a person who is not stressed about something. Everyone, right from little kids to retired elderly, is living a stressful life nowadays. Little kids are stressed about their school and friends, adults about work and politics, the elderly about their purpose and existence in general. Being stressed about things is normal; in fact, many people proclaim that they perform really well when they are stressed about something. But being stressed all the time can wreak havoc on your mind as well as body. Stress can lead to various mental and physical disorders, many of which are life-threatening.

Stress is often accompanied by anxiety. The number of people suffering from anxiety disorders is on the rise since the last couple of decades. Anxiety is harmful to your personal, professional, and social life, as well. People who suffer from anxiety disorders often cannot perform well. Many great and highly talented artists could not achieve and fulfill their potential just because they suffered from anxiety. Stress combined with anxiety can break a person completely and shatter his dreams and plans.

While there are many different treatments and methods available today that can help you tackle anxiety and stress, but many of these involve medication. These medicines are costly and are often unavailable. They also have many harmful side effects. This is why many people who suffer from these problems often become discouraged and lost.

But don't worry; it is possible to get rid of these problems without medications with the help of Buddhism. Many people have now started looking at Buddhism as a way to attain a peaceful mind and a tranquil life. But understanding Buddhism is not easy. It is one of the most ancient religions and schools of philosophy in the world, which has deep-set roots in ancient Indian cultures. A lot of people have left Buddhism before because they could not understand it leading to confusion and frustration. If you are one of those people, congratulations, you have finally unlocked the secret of understanding, Buddhism is a simple and lucid manner.

What makes this book one of the best books on Buddhism is the fact that it can be read by anyone. While specifically meant for beginners, this book is also useful for people who understand Buddhism and have practiced it for a long time. This book is easy to understand and contains all the necessary information that is required to begin your path towards Buddhism. This book has been prepared by consulting many reputed sources regarding Buddhism and simplifying the vast knowledge contained in Buddhist scriptures. It breaks down the complex concept of Buddhism and deconstructs it so that even the most novice reader can understand its principles and doctrine.

This book is recommended for everyone who wants to gain a clear yet concise understanding of Buddhism. It covers all the basics of Buddhism in sufficient detail. Buddhism is a brilliant way of living life as, unlike other religions, it forces you to look for the source of your problems inside you. This introspective quality of Buddhism is often compared to modern-day psychology. Thus, it can be safely assumed that Buddhism is based on science. This book provides you with different codes of practice, which, if you incorporate in your life, can change it for good.

Buddhism has become really popular in the modern world. Many famous thinkers, rationalists, entrepreneurs, etc. are Buddhists. For instance, Leonard Cohen, Orlando Bloom, Steve Jobs, Jack Kerouac, Allen Ginsberg, Penelope Cruz, Jet Li, Courtney Love, Richard Gere, George Takei, Sharon Stone, Naomi Watts, Tina Turner, and many other successful people are Buddhists. Many of them credit Buddhism to be one of the reasons why they are successful.

The success of the above-mentioned people is not due to some divine intervention; rather, it is due to the various practices and exercises that are prescribed in Buddhism. These exercises are mentioned in detail in this book. Like the above-mentioned people, if you incorporate these exercises in your daily life, you too will start noticing positive changes in yourself, your life, and the atmosphere around you as well.

Stress is a slow killer. It doesn't just affect your personal life, but it can also ruin the lives of people around you. Stress is also bad for your professional life. But the worst thing stress can do make your life unlivable. People who are stressed and anxious all the time hate their lives because they cannot find peace in it. Such people often start using drugs and may even contemplate suicide as well. If you are one of such people who feel that their life has no pleasure or peace, you need to act right now. Choosing the path of Buddha can change your life for good. It will allow you to feel peace and pleasure once again.

Don't worry; you do not need to become a Buddhist to enjoy its fruits. Buddhism is a flexible philosophy that can be incorporated into your present beliefs as well.

Wake up and start waking on the path laid by Buddha now! Good luck!

Chapter One: An Overview of Buddhism

Before moving on to the various practices of Buddhism, it is crucial to understand its basics. This chapter will try to answer all the basic questions that you may have about Buddha and Buddhism.

What do Buddhists Believe?

This is a difficult question to answer, as Buddhism is not an organized religion like the Abrahamic ones. Buddhism is often said to be a living organism composed of many different religions, sects, and ideas that live together like a huge family. Buddhism developed over hundreds of years in many different parts of the world; the growth hasn't stopped. Each sect, group, and often individual interprets Buddhism differently.

While all the sects of Buddhism are different in some way, all of them are linked to each other by the tenets and practices laid down by Buddha, an Indian prince who changed the course of the world. Buddha lived in India sometime between the fourth and sixth centuries BCE and taught many different things, which later became the basis of Buddhism. Buddha was not his real name and was given to him when he became enlightened. Buddha means 'awakened one.' He was able to release himself from the cycle of samsara, i.e., the cycle of pain and rebirth. Buddha attained enlightenment and found unconditional and everlasting happiness. Nothing could disturb it, including illness, old age, or even death. Buddha preached and taught about this path throughout his life to help others achieve the same freedom from samsara.

Buddha preached that suffering and dissatisfaction, illness, old age, and death are all important and inseparable parts of life and are unavoidable. However, suffering is our own creation. Suffering is a result of clinging and attachment. We desire things to stay or be in a certain way, and when they do not remain so, we suffer. Buddha preached that every action and idea has consequences, forming a never-ending chain. This is often called the chain of karma.

It is crucial to understand that we are the creators of our suffering. Similarly, with efforts, we can end this suffering as well. Every person on this Earth has the capacity to exit the cycle of rebirth and suffering.

People who are not born into a Buddhist family often pick up Buddhism through various methods. Learning about the teachings of Buddha and understanding and witnessing the practices of Buddhism is often a gateway for people to Buddhism. Conversations with Buddhists, meditation, and even books like this can help you start your study of Buddhism.

While many major schools and sects of Buddhism offer formal conversion or transition ceremonies, they are not crucial. Your practice, faith, and dedication towards the teachings of Buddha make you a Buddhist. In formal ceremonies, the inductee is taught 'Trisharana' or the 'three shelters.' A person can take shelter from the vicissitudes of life in these three shelters. These shelters are Buddha (the physical embodiment), the Dhamma (the teachings), and the Sangha (the community). These three together are also called as 'Triratna' or triple gems or jewels.

Is Buddhism a Religion, a Philosophy, or a Way of Life?

Buddhism is one of the most complex practices in the world, and it is difficult to define it. Buddhism can be defined as a combination of philosophy, religion, and a way of life. It depends on the practitioner and the student how he or she interprets it. It is possible to study Buddhism in a purely philosophical way, as well.

Many practitioners think of Buddhism as a religion. As mentioned earlier, Buddhism is considered to be a living family of religions with different philosophical sects and aspects. One of the major things that people find attractive about Buddhism is its deep philosophy. Buddhism does not ask you to believe in things blindly; rather, it asks you to investigate your mind, reality, and reason. It is one of the few religions that promote critical thinking as well as reasoning. This is due to its philosophical base.

Buddhism has an end-goal, which is to find a release from the cycle of pain and rebirth. This end-goal makes Buddhism a form of religion. Buddhism offers a path to escape from this cycle with the help of ethics and different practices. Other elements of Buddhism can also be considered to be religious. Each sect and school of Buddhism has developed different rights, rituals, books, etc. They express their devotion to Buddha in many different ways, as well.

Certain characteristics of Buddhism do not match the typical ideas of religion. For instance, there is no divine revelation in Buddhism. Similarly, practitioners are not required to read scriptures and attend regular services. The scriptures are not considered to be the absolute truth, like, for instance, the Bible or the Holy Quran. Buddhism does not encourage a leap of faith and makes you question everything.

Practitioners rarely get into debates regarding the true nature of Buddhism. For them, Buddhism is just a way of escaping the world of pain. Often Buddhism is compared with western notions of religion, which is why people find it phony and unreal. Buddhism is concerned with meaning and not doctrine.

Who was Buddha?

Buddha, before becoming Buddha, was an Indian prince named Siddhartha Gautama. Born in Lumbini, Nepal, Siddhartha lived around 2600 years ago in the northern region of India and Nepal. Siddhartha was a prince and thus a warrior. He was born in the Shakya clan to King Shuddhodhana and Queen Maya. Buddha is often known as Shakyamuni, which means the Sage of Shakyas.

There are many legends and stories associated with the birth of Siddhartha. According to some legends, the birth of Buddha was prophesied by a great sage who told his father that the child would either grow up to become a 'Chakravathi' or the king of the world or will become a world-renowned spiritual leader. Shuddhodhana was shocked to hear these words and did everything in his power to stop his son from becoming spiritual. He surrounded and showered Siddhartha with luxuries, privileges, and all the joys of the mortal world and sheltered him from all the harsh realities outside the palace. Siddhartha thus grew up to be a pampered prince who did not understand pain and suffering. He was married off to an intelligent princess called Yashodhara, who soon bore him a son called Rahula. When Rahula was still young, the prince managed to escape the palace and witness something that changed his life forever.

Siddhartha witnessed the truth of life when he escaped his palace. While riding in a carriage, he saw a sick man in immense pain. In his next ride, he saw an old, tired man. In the third ride, he saw a funeral procession and understood that death was inevitable. These three encounters were his first experience of the inevitable suffering of human beings. On his next ride, Siddhartha saw a mendicant meditating and realized that he could to find a way out of this cycle of suffering.

Soon after these encounters, Siddhartha, at the tender age of 29, left his palace, wife, son, and all the materialistic pleasures of this world and set on a quest to find the true meaning and release from the cycle of suffering. He studied, meditated, met with many people, and fasted for many years. He soon realized that exiting the cycle of pain was possible only with the help of the 'middle way.' Extremities of any sort would not help him to escape samsara. A person who indulges in extreme material pleasures is similar to a person who indulges in extreme physical denial. Siddhartha realized that the only way to end suffering was the 'middle way,' which could be achieved by training your mind. He then decided to meditate under a Ficus tree (Peepal or Bodhi tree) in a small town called Bodhgaya in north India. For 49 days, he meditated and received many insights into the nature of reality, and finally, after a long struggle, he became enlightened. The existence of Prince Siddhartha vanished, and Buddha emerged. For the next 45 years, Buddha preached and taught the path of freedom that he had realized under the Bodhi tree.

Siddhartha's life of spirituality was not an easy one. Soon after leaving his palace, he spent around six years practicing and studying under different teachers. These teachers had many different methods of meditation, often extreme and sometimes inhumane. While these meditations helped him get away from the palace, he understood that these were otherwise useless- he could not achieve his goal, which was freedom from the samsara.

According to Buddhist traditions, the first people Buddha taught were his five companions, spiritual seekers. Siddhartha had practiced severe self-denial with them and had then abandoned the practice.

These five seekers met Buddha near Benares in India and tried to avoid him, for they thought that he had gone back to the life of luxury. However, soon, they realized that the old Siddhartha had vanished and had become Buddha. Buddha then taught them the 'middle path' and said that neither self-indulgence nor self-denial could help them in their goal. This is the Middle Way or the Maddhyama Marga. Later Buddha taught these men the foundational bases of Buddhism, including Chatura Arya Satya or four noble truths and the Ashtanga Marga or the eight-fold path. Thus, the Sangha was born, and Buddhism began.

Over the next 45 years, Buddha managed to reach out to thousands of people from every walk of life.

People from all castes, creeds, class, gender, etc. became students of Buddha. Even murderers and hardened criminals were accepted in the Sangha. Prince Siddhartha's family, including his son, wife, and father, too, joined the Sangha.

Many of Buddha's students became enlightened and spread his message. Sariputta, Moggallana, Mahakasyapa, etc. were some of his star students. Mahakasyapa is said to have organized the First Council of Buddhism after the death of Buddha. In this council, 500 enlightened monks gathered and discussed and collected Buddha's sermons.

According to certain texts, women were not allowed to join the monastic communities in the beginning, and only men were allowed to become bhikkhus or monks. Buddha's stepmother, Mahapajapati, and a council of 500 other women approached Buddha and requested him to grant them permission to join. Buddha's disciple Ananda too, requested him to grant women permission to join the sangha. Women were soon allowed to become bhikkunis. According to some sources, this story is false, and women were allowed to join sangha right from the beginning.

Buddha's Death

Buddha's death is considered to be as important as his life. After 45 years of teaching, Buddha passed away at the age of 80. He was surrounded by a large group of students when he died smiling. This event is also known as Mahaparinirvana. Buddha had escaped samsara and was free from the cycle of death, birth, and suffering.

According to early Pali texts, three months after the Mahaparinirvana, around 400 BCE, the First Buddhist Council took place. Here around 500 senior, enlightened monks gathered and discussed the teachings of Buddha and planned how his teachings should be preserved.

Seventy years after Mahaparinirvana, another council was held. In this council, certain disputed rules regarding bhikkhus and bhikkhus were discussed. Here the sangha underwent dramatic change and got divided into two branches. One of these branches wanted to uphold all the traditional rules of Buddha's teachings, while the other wanted to move on with time and relax certain rules.

It is said that a third council was held during the reign of Emperor Asoka, one of the most celebrated rulers of India. Emperor Asoka became a Buddhist around 250 BCE after witnessing a massacre. Emperor Asoka is responsible for spreading Buddhism across the subcontinent- even Asia. The third council was held to remove corruption from the sangha. Heretics were banned from the sangha as well. Many essential components of the Buddhist scriptures were discussed and formalized in this council. In the third council, Emperor Asoka decided to send teaching missions around the subcontinent to spread the word of Buddha. These emissaries took Buddha's teachings to Sri Lanka, Myanmar, Himalayas, etc. In later years Buddhism spread over East and Southeast Asia and beyond.

Origin of Buddhism

The origin of Buddhism is a complex and sometimes controversial topic. In this section, let us have a look at its inception and history.

Buddhism is followed by more than 300 million people around the world. Yet, Buddhism is quite different than any other religion as almost all sects of Buddhism deny a supreme deity. For Buddhists, the teachings of Buddha hold the supreme position. The earliest form of Buddhism was thoroughly based on the teachings of Buddha. Here it was believed that through proper moral code, efforts, dedication, and action, anyone could achieve enlightenment. This form of Buddhism is still practiced (albeit in a slightly altered form). This form of Buddhism is called the Hinayana or Theravada Buddhism. Theravada means the Way of the Elders. This form is practiced in most of Southeast Asia.

Another prominent school of Buddhism is the Mahayana or the Great Vehicle. Its inception can be traced to the first century CE. In this Buddhism, Buddha became a deity, and soon other past and future Buddha's as well as Bodhisattvas were added to the pantheon. Bodhisattvas are enlightened people who postpone their nirvana just so that they can help others on the path of salvation. Mahayana Buddhism is popular in Central Asia and Far East Asia.

Another form of Buddhism developed in the seventh century CE were different practices, doctrines and esoteric dogma got mixed with Buddhism. Necromancy from Hindu beliefs got added to Buddhism as well. This form of Buddhism is called the Tantrism or Vajrayana Buddhism (the Diamond Path). It became extremely popular in the Himalayan regions, and soon, female Bodhisattvas were added to the already expanded pantheon of Buddhism. It is here mandala, and similar cosmic patterns were added to Buddhism. Many local beliefs, shamanic, and sometimes terrifying deities were added to Buddhism, and a new religion was born. Unlike other forms of Buddhism, in Vajrayana, a spiritual teacher or guru is essential to guide on the path of nirvana.

Thus, the origin of Buddhism is convoluted. You will find out more about the schools of Buddhism later in this chapter.

Buddhist Texts and Scriptures

Many religions of the world have particular scriptures that are considered to be holy and the word of God. However, there are no particular or specific texts that are considered to the ultimate Book of Religion. This is due to the fact that Buddhism is a living family of many different spiritual and philosophical systems. No single set of scriptures is considered to be authoritative by all the Buddhist sects and groups. Each Buddhist sect has its own textual canon that it follows.

Theravada or the Way of the Elders Buddhists follow the Pali canon. This canon contains some of the oldest Buddhist texts. This canon is known as the Pali canon because many of its books are in an ancient Indian language called Pali. These scriptures are known as Tipitaka, which means Three Baskets. These include the 'Sutta Pitaka,' the 'Vinaya Pitaka,' and the 'Abhidhamma Pitaka.' Sutta means sutras, which are the discourses of Buddha and some of his major students. The Vinaya Pitaka contains a code of discipline for the monks, and the Abhidhamma Pitaka contains a detailed study of the origin, nature, and the interaction of psychological and material phenomena. These texts are dated sometime between the third and the first century BCE.

East Asian Buddhist sects present in Japan, Korea, China, and Vietnam follow the Chinese canon. The texts present in this canon can be dated back to the first century BCE to the fifth century CE. There exists a lot of overlap between the Pali and the Chinese canons. Doctrines and methods are the distinguishing features of the Chinese canon. Another canon that often overlaps the Chinese canon is the Tibetan canon. The Tibetan canon contains two parts, the Kangyur or the word of Buddha and the Tengyur, the later commentaries. Tibetan canon also contains various tantric rituals and descriptions.

Certain branches of Buddhism like to base the practices on certain treatises or sutras only. For instance, Nichiren Buddhism is based around the Lotus Sutra and chanting its title is an integral part of the practice. Another branch, the Pure Land Buddhists, practice the three sutras that are focused on Bodhisattva Amitabha or Amitabha Buddha, i.e.,

Buddha of Infinite Light. This Buddha is supposed to reign over 'the pure land.' This pure land is often referred to as the Buddhist heaven by these practitioners.

Buddhism and Reincarnation

Reincarnation is an integral part of Buddhism, as Buddha believed that any living being is caught in the cycle of samsara. In this cycle, a living being is born, then he or she dies, and ultimately is reborn. To escape this cycle of samsara and pain is enlightenment.

According to Buddhist texts, people are reborn because of desire and clinging. As said earlier, desire is also the root cause of suffering. So ultimately, desire and suffering are the reasons behind samsara. Buddha believed that every clinging adds a brick to the bridge of the next life.

Buddha said that when, where, and how a person will be reborn solely depends on the karma or the credit that he or she accumulated in his or her past life. This means our deeds in previous and this life affect our next life. He believed that even at the time of death and later, we could make certain choices that can affect our next birth, whether positively or negatively. Buddhists believe that the attitude of mind at the time of death is crucial. If we are calm, focused, and pleased while dying, we will be born in good circumstances. Thus, preparing yourself for death through meditation forms an integral part of the Buddhist practice.

There are many different ideas about what happens at and after death in Buddhism. These ideas differ from tradition to tradition. For instance, many branches of Buddhism believe that chanting certain parts of some scriptures and holy mantras can help the dying in the next life. Many Buddhist texts also name and describe various realms like heaven and hell. In certain scriptures, these are thought to be the creation of the dying mind.

Many secular and modern Buddhists do not believe in reincarnation and rebirth. Such Buddhists mostly focus on the secular aspects of Buddhism, including meditation and mindfulness. Many secular Buddhists compare themselves with the early Buddhists, as they did not believe in God and similar principles as well. Yet, there is a huge difference between the two- the modern do not believe in reincarnation and new births while the early Buddhists did believe in these.

Understanding the basics of any philosophy or religion is crucial as it reduces confusion. In the next chapter, let us have a look at different sects of Buddhism that are currently practiced in the world.

Chapter Two: The Schools of Buddhism

In the last chapter, different schools and sects of Buddhism were introduced briefly. In this chapter, let us have a close look at some of the most prominent schools of Buddhism.

There are a variety of schools or sects of Buddhism thanks to its inclusive nature. The two principal forms of Buddhism are Theravada Buddhism that is prominently present in Cambodia, Sri Lanka, Thailand, Myanmar, Laos, etc. and the Mahayana Buddhism, which is dominant in China, Japan, Taiwan, Mongolia, and Korea. A version of the Mahayana Buddhism, often known as the Tibetan or Vajrayana Buddhism is dominant in Tibet and surrounding Himalaya region. The practices and doctrines of all the branches of Buddhism may be different; however, all of them are focused on helping the practitioner to follow the path of enlightenment. Almost none of the Buddhist sects focus on conversion except the Nichiren Buddhism in Japan.

The three main branches of Buddhism developed over a long period of time. Each of these has its own spiritual ideals and characteristics. Hinayana or the Lesser Vehicle is often called foundational Buddhism. It is the precursor of the Theravada school. This school emphasizes enlightenment through monastic life. Not many people follow this school now. In fact, the word Hinayana was coined by the Mahayana sect and is seen to be a pejorative. Mahayana Buddhists call it a difficult path and thus a lesser path because very few people can follow it.

Many sects believe that you need multiple lives to reach enlightenment except Vajrayana Buddhism. The Vajrayana or the Tibetan Buddhists believe that it is possible to achieve enlightenment in a single life without having to accumulate enough good karma in past lives.

The three major branches of Buddhism are not mutually exclusive, and they often overlap. However, their different practices and doctrines have made Buddhism and Buddhist art a complex structure.

Foundational or the Hinayana Buddhists believe that enlightenment can only be achieved by monks and that too through their own efforts. Mahayana and Vajrayana, on the other hand, believe that everyone can become a Buddha with the help of Bodhisattvas. Due to this, Mahayana and Vajrayana Buddhists often have many shrines dedicated to these Bodhisattvas and Buddha's. They also form an integral part of their art.

As said earlier, the oldest form of Buddhism (for the common people) is called Theravada. In this form, the practitioners strictly adhere to the teachings of Buddha and often lead a life of meditation. Practitioners believe that only a few people can reach nirvana with ample efforts. In this form of Buddhism, initially, Buddha was not represented in human form; instead, various symbols and icons were used. At the beginning of the first century, under the able rule of Kushana kings, Buddha began to be presented in human form. Around the same time, Mahayana, a new branch of Buddhism, arose. For Mahayana Buddhists, Buddha is much more than a teacher and a human being; he is a savior god. They believe that Buddha appeared on this earth in the perfect human form so that he could guide and help people achieve nirvana.

Theravada Buddhism

Theravada Buddhism is also known as the Buddhism or doctrine of the elders. It is considered to be the oldest out of all three prominent schools of Buddhism. It is also the most orthodox out of the three. Theravada practitioners believe that their doctrine is the closest to what Shakyamuni Buddha taught and preached. Their practices, beliefs, and doctrines are based on the recollections of Buddha's teachings, which were collected by Buddha's companions. These companions are known as Elders. They were the senior-most and highly respected monks. Nowadays, Theravada is predominantly practiced in Thailand, Sri Lanka, Myanmar, Laos, Cambodia, and certain parts of Vietnam. A lot of practitioners can be found in India as well.

Theravada was not the only school of Buddhism that existed after the death of Buddha. In fact, around 18 prominent schools of Buddhism practiced their religion and philosophy in harmony. Many other schools of Buddhism disappeared with attacks from various other religions.

For the followers of Theravada Buddhism, the enlightenment of the individual, spirituality, pure deeds and thoughts, self-discipline, etc. are important. They think that monastic life and following the rules of ancient Vinaya is essential as well. Theravada Buddhism prescribes specific roles and rules for monks and common people. In Theravada Buddhism, each person is responsible for her or his own nirvana. It also believes that only a monk can attain nirvana.

Theravada Buddhism Beliefs

Theravada Buddhism holds many beliefs that often overlap with other forms of Buddhism. In Theravada Buddhism, the three Noble Virtues are as follows:

- Dukkha or Suffering, pain, and pursuit of desire.

- Annica or the temporary state of being and all things

- Annata or the illusion that is known as reality

Theravada Buddhists believe that everything is temporary, and if you get attached to material things, it will only lead to unhappiness and suffering. It will also interfere in spiritual matters. Annica teaches that nothing is permanent. If you try to focus on states of mind, experiences, objects, materialistic pleasure, it will only lead to dukkha. Annata understands that there is no point in considering these things important and necessary.

Theravada Buddhism does not allow practitioners to worship any living or nonliving objects. The offerings of flowers and fruits in shrines are not considered to be an object of worship; rather, they are seen as symbols of impermanence. Similarly, chanting is only the reminder of the teachings of Buddha, the Dhamma, and the Sangha.

According to Theravada Buddhists, Gautama Buddha was a human being and not a divine figure, a deity, or a legend. He experienced the same sufferings and pains that all of us experience. What made him unique was that he wanted to transcend beyond this pain and suffering. It is said that Buddha took a vow in front of the first-ever Buddha that he would reincarnate many times and finally become a Buddha. Theravada Buddhists believe that the death or Mahaparinirvana of Buddha is his escape from the human world.

Mahayana stresses on becoming a Bodhisattva. Buddha never gave any explicit instructions on how one should become a

Bodhisattva. All the information regarding is collected in many sutras; however, these sutras were written after Mahaparinirvana. When he was alive, Buddha majorly focused on how to end suffering in one's current life and achieve "Arhatship." Theravada Buddhists thus believe their practices to be purer and closer to what Buddha preached.

Buddha referred to himself as Arhat multiple times, which has led to a lot of confusion in scholars and practitioners as well. Arhat in Pali means 'perfected person' or a person who has achieved Nirvana. Buddha calling himself an Arhat implies that he was no different than his enlightened students. What made him different was that he had mastered everything that is associated with enlightenment. This is why Mahayana Buddhists often believe that total enlightenment should be postponed until one becomes perfect.

Most of Mahayana's knowledge is based on the Lotus Sutra, which was taken from the Nagas by Nagarjuna. Nagarjuna is considered to be the second greatest master after Buddha himself by many. Many people also believe that Nagarjuna was, in fact, a new Buddha who was born to clarify any doubts that the past Buddha might have left. You will find more information regarding Nagarjuna later in this chapter.

As said earlier, Mahayana Buddhists stress on becoming Bodhisattva. This stress was the main reason behind the strain between Mahayana and Theravada Buddhist schools. Avalokiteshvara is considered to be the highest Bodhisattva who stalled his enlightenment just because he wanted everyone to be enlightened first. Many Mahayana shrines are dedicated to Avalokiteshvara.

Mahayana Buddhism has many different sects, practices, and philosophical schools under its shelter. A said earlier,

Mahayana is more popular and widespread than other forms of Buddhism throughout the world. It includes many different and modern forms of Buddhism, including Soka-Gakkai and Zen.

Mahayana means a great vehicle because Buddhist philosophy compares itself to a vehicle that will carry people from the world of pain and suffering. It's known as greater because, unlike other schools, Mahayana is all-encompassing (according to the followers).

The main reason why Mahayana became so widespread and popular was that it allowed the monks to travel more freely. Along with this, the concept of Bodhisattva, which was similar to many local religions and pantheon, was easily accepted by the people.

Mahayana Buddhism Beliefs

Mahayana Buddhists believe that there exist many different kinds of heavens, hell, and nirvana. Bodhisattvas enjoy an exalted status in Mahayana because they help others in achieving nirvana by stalling their own.

Mahayana Buddhism tenets are comparatively vague and 'universal' than the strict codes of Theravada Buddhism. They believe that anyone can achieve nirvana. They love philosophical discussions and are often seen debating and discussing various topics. They worship many male and female deities along with a large pantheon of gods, Bodhisattvas, and Buddhas.

For Mahayana Buddhists, Buddha was a magical and divine figure who was born on the earth to help mankind. The

Supreme Buddha became an omniscient force like a creator God.

Differences Between Mahayana Buddhist and Theravada Buddhists

The distinction between Theravada Buddhism and Mahayana Buddhism is often confusing because they overlap a lot. In this section, let us have a close look at the differences between these two branches of Buddhism.

Mahayana practitioners believe that they have just expanded on the beliefs of Theravada Buddhists and that their doctrines are still based on the teachings of Buddha. The Theravada followers believe that Mahayana is a corrupted form and also view it to be too easy. Theravada Buddhists firmly believe that only your own efforts can help you achieve salvation, while the Mahayana Buddhists think that faith and help from Bodhisattvas can help them achieve salvation.

The concept of Bodhisattvas is where the Mahayana doctrines and Theravada doctrines differ vastly. Mahayana Buddhists believe that there exist many Bodhisattvas as well as many Buddha's. Theravada Buddhists believe that there was just one Buddha and Bodhisattva, Buddha himself.

Tantric Buddhism

Tibetan, Tantric, or Vajrayana Buddhism is a branch of Mahayana Buddhism, which has become a full-fledged tree in its own right. It began with the Tibetan Buddhist monks around the early seventh century CE. Tantric or esoteric Buddhists accept the tenets prescribed by Mahayana monks but also added different forms of mediation guided by gurus and masters. These meditations often involve magical words, mantras, symbols, and practices that are said to speed up the process of achieving enlightenment.

Tibetan Buddhists believe that with ample compassion and meditation, people can achieve nirvana in one single life. These practices and beliefs developed parallel to Hindu practices and beliefs. Due to this, many different and new deities appeared in their pantheon. These deities are of different genders and are represented in different gestures, poses, expressions, etc. Certain deities are also wrathful, and they represent protection. Another major idea in Esoteric Buddhism is the concept of five celestial Buddha's. These five Buddha's each represent a direction, and the last one represents zenith.

It is often called a syncretic mix of Mahayana doctrines with local pantheistic religions and Tantra. The Bon religion has had an immense influence on Tibetan Buddhism. All the activities such as public practices, prayers, etc. are organized and handled by monasteries and temples. Lamas are considered to be the religious heads of the Tibetan Buddhist communities.

Tantrism is a highly ritualistic religion that originated in India. It believes in esoteric philosophy along with magic. Many different sacred shapes, chants, techniques, etc. are used in regular practice in this school of Buddhism.

As said earlier, the ancient Bon religion has had an immense influence on Tibetan Buddhism. For instance, Tibetan Buddhist practices like shamans, dispelling demons, pleasing gods, different mudras, mantras, yantras, and the practice of secret initiation have all been taken from the Bon religion. Mudras are ritual postures; mantras are special words; yantras are special symbols such as the mandala, etc. A lot of symbols, images, objects, etc. of deities worshiped in Tibetan Buddhism have been borrowed or derived from Tantrism. Many of the practices and techniques associated with this school of Buddhism were passed down orally.

The inception of Tantrism can be traced back to 600 CE in India. It was based on texts that are known as Tantras. According to Tantrism, all human conditions, states, feelings, etc. are connected, which means desire, anger, love, hope, etc. are all similar. According to many scholars, Tantrism is a complex combination of Buddhism and Hinduism. It combines Buddhist philosophy, with local folklore and legends and incorporated Hindu gods in its teachings. The erotic and charged Hindu ideas were mixed with authoritative and static teachings of Buddha to form Tantrism.

Why did Buddhism get Divided?

There are many theories behind why Buddhism broke into many factions. According to one theory, a couple of centuries after the death of Buddha, the atmosphere of sangha started heating up over politics. The members could not decide who would run the sangha and whether anyone should run it or not. Another controversy regarding certain rules pertaining to monks created a strain. A handful of Arhats made some decisions that angered a significant number of monks who resented how a small number of Arhats could influence the affairs of the monastery. Disgruntled, the monks and many other disciples worked for many years to lower the status of Arhats, and instead, the Bodhisattva was brought forward to be the ideal.

Mahayana branch of Buddhism still follows most of the original teachings of Buddha, but many of these teachings have undergone a lot of interpolation throughout the years. The Chinese Mahayana, which is most dominant in Taiwan, is considerably similar to the older Mahayana sect, while the Mahayana of Vietnam, Japan, and Korea are later developments. The Mahayana of Tibet is so different than the original Mahayana that now it is considered to be a different branch of Buddhism itself.

Nagarjuna

In the modern world, many people follow the Mahayana way of Buddhism. It is perhaps the most prominent form of Buddhism that is extant today. It is, therefore, necessary to have a deeper look at Mahayana. To understand the development of Mahayana and its philosophy, it is necessary to study its greatest teacher (after Buddha) Nagarjuna. In this section, let us have a brief introduction of Nagarjuna and his work.

Nagarjuna was born around 150 CE. He is often regarded as the second Buddha about whom the first Buddha prophesized. Nagarjuna did clarify a lot of things and created the Heart Sutra.

Nagarjuna is considered to be the most important Mahayana philosopher and thinker. He, along with his disciple Aryadev founded the Madhyamaka school of Mahayana Buddhism. Nagarjuna also developed the Prajnaparamita sutras. According to a legend, he brought these texts from the Nagas or divine snakes. He also wrote many treatises on Rasayana and was the head of the Nalanda University for many years.

Not a lot is known about the life of Nagarjuna, and whatever information we have is from legends, accounts, and sometimes myths written about him in China and Tibet many years after his death. According to certain legends, Nagarjuna was born in South India and was an advisor of a Satavahana (an ancient Indian dynasty) king. According to other sources, Nagarjuna was a Brahman from the Vidarbha region in the western state of Maharashtra in India.

Nagarjuna Writing and Philosophy

A large number of important Buddhist texts are attributed to Nagarjuna; however, many of these claims have little to no evidence to back them up. Even today, a huge debate continues regarding his contribution to Buddhism. However, everyone agrees that Nagarjuna definitely wrote the Mulamadhyamakakarika (Fundamental Verses on the Middle Way). According to other sources Nagarjuna wrote Sunyatasaptati (Seventy Verses on Emptiness); Mulamadhyamaka-karika (Fundamental Verses of the Middle Way); Vyavaharasiddhi (Proof of Convention); Yuktiaika (Sixty Verses on Reasoning); Bodhicittavivaraa (Exposition of the Enlightened Mind); Vigrahavyavartani (The End of Disputes); Catustava (Hymn to the Absolute Reality); Vaidalyaprakaraa (Pulverizing the Categories); Bodhisabhara (Requisites of Enlightenment); Ratnavali (Precious Garland); Suhllekha (Letter to a Good Friend); and Pratityasamutpadahdayakarika (Constituents of Dependent Arising).

Nagarjuna was well aware of many sects, religions, Sravaka philosophies, etc. that existed in his times. He was a scholar of gigantic merit. He was mainly focused on the concept of Shunyata or emptiness.

Other Schools of Buddhism

Zen and the Ch'an Sect of Buddhism

The Ch'an sect, also known as the Ching'T'u sect, is often described as the faith of wisdom. It inspired the Zen school of Buddhism in Japan. Ch'an stands for meditation. Its four main principles are:

- A special transmission outside of the doctrines

- The written word is not an authority

- Pointing at the heart of man directly

- Understanding one's nature and becoming a Buddha

The origins of this sect cannot be traced, as they are confusing and unclear. Some people believe that the early leaders of this sect were mythical/legendary, while others believe that they were real. Ch'an truly became a distinct sect when its sixth patriarch Hui-Neng spent around 15 years meditating in hills.

Zen Buddhism is a distinct version of the Ch'an School. It was brought to Japan from China in the reign of the Chinese Sung Dynasty around the 10th century by a Chinese monk called Huineng. Zen was not a popular sect in the beginning; however, in the 12th century, it became popular rapidly.

The aesthetics of Ch'an has had a great impact on East Asian art. Ch'an artists did not care for symmetry and figures present in the Sino-Indian tradition. For them trying to get as much as possible from each shade or line was essential. For them, art became a contemplative exercise, and for the viewers, it turned into a form of meditation.

School of Pure Land

The School of Pure Land, also known as the School of Pure Thought in Japan, is another Chinese school of Buddhism that has many practitioners all over the world. Its inception can be traced back to 500 CE. It started as a form of worship of Amitabha Buddha, Buddha of the Western paradise. What makes this form of Buddhism different than the Ch'an School is that it focuses and strongly recommends idolatry. The School of Pure Land is not as strong as the Ch'an School in China; however, it has significant practitioners all over Japan.

In the School of Pure Land form of Buddhism, the Mahayana belief of Bodhisattvas and Buddha is taken further. They believe that the Bodhisattva can help people attain nirvana who otherwise would have never succeeded in doing so. The importance of Bodhisattvas and numerous Buddha's is seen through a variety of descriptions of them in Pure Land shrines as well as caves.

According to certain scholars, the School of Pure Land started in India; however, as the oldest surviving texts of this sect are in Chinese and not in an Indian language, this claim cannot be proven. Others believe that it was founded by Hui Yuan, a Chinese monk. While the beginning of this sect cannot be traced, its presence and growth in China were considerable. When it started growing popular in China, Bodhisattvas were given Chinese names, and the arts and aesthetics changed as well.

Thus, these are some of the most prominent and studied sects and schools of Buddhism that are currently extant in the world. As it is clear that while the sects differ on many counts, the teachings of Buddha still form the basic core of all of them, thus uniting them under the name of Buddhism. Many different practices have risen from the above-mentioned schools. Some of these practices have adopted the secular aspects of Buddhism to preach mental and physical health.

Chapter Three: Buddhism- Other Concepts

Buddhism is a complex philosophy with many concepts that may confuse beginners; in this chapter, let us have a brief look at some of the major and important aspects of Buddhism.

Mind

The mind is a complex concept in philosophy and science. Western scientists are still confused about the function and nature of mind and consciousness. Even the existence of the mind is debatable. Buddhism, however, believes that the mind exists and explains it extensively. These explanations still stand true after 2000 years. In this section, let us have a look at these explanations.

As said earlier, the mind is a complex concept. The Pali word for the mind cannot be directly translated and compared with the English word mind as the intricacies and details get lost in translation. To understand the concept, we need to look at the different parts of the mind that are explained in the suttas.

According to the suttas, the mind consists of the following parts.

- Citta
- Mano
- Vinnana

These three are the crucial components that one needs to study and understand while looking for nirvana. Let us have a look at all the above concepts one by one.

Citta

Citta is often translated as the mind in English; however, at some places, it is also translated as the heart. For instance, in Dhammapada, at some places, 'mettacitta' is translated as a loving heart. An entire section of the Dhammapada called the Cittavagga is concerned with Citta, which proves how crucial the concept is for Buddhism.

So what does Citta mean?

Citta is a mind that has a certain quality. For instance, you may come across words such as cittapassaddhi meaning serene mind, mettacitta meaning loving heart, cittasaṅkhāraṃ meaning conditioned the mind, vimuttacittaṃ meaning released mind, ariyacittassa meaning noble mind and anāsavacittassa meaning taint-less mind, in Buddhism. Thus it is clear that citta can have quality. Citta indicates the mental state.

Mano

The next crucial word related to the mind is mano. Citta is slightly easier to translate; however, translating mano in English is difficult.

One can find words like dummano or unhappy mind, attamano or delighted mind, sumano or glad mind, manopadosa or ill-willed mind, manovitakka or thoughts, manopubbangama or something that is directed by the mind, manobhavaniyassa or the respect for the mind, manosoceyyam or purity of mind, manoduccaritena of bad mentality and manosucaritena or right efforts in Buddhist scriptures.

The Relation between Mano and Citta

All three concepts of the mind are related. It is possible to find the relationship between Citta and mano in the Mahaparinibbana sutta. It shows how everything has a cause, and the feelings that we get from an object or event are ultimately related to the cause. These feelings affect our citta/mind. This is known as dependent origination.

Vinnana

The third word that is associated with the concept of mind is vinnana. Vinnana is often translated as consciousness in English. Consciousness is based on manovinnana or the senses of the mind. The rise and fall of vinnana, the relationship of vinnana, and other parts of the mind all are explained in detail in many Buddhist suttas.

Using the above three concepts, the concept of mind in Buddhism can be explained as follows:

Consciousness is based on stimulus, and if the stimulus is removed, the consciousness is lost. This is the first aspect of the mind. Our consciousness leads to various mental impressions. These impressions are part of mano. Mano and vinnana both have an effect on the overall condition of the mind. This overall state is known as citta.

Liberation and the Mind

The vinnana aspect of the mind is often unsatisfied. By observing and understanding this dissatisfaction, one can achieve liberation. When you are not attached to the vinnana, the mano will not function. When the mano ceases to function, the citta will automatically stop changing. Thus the citta is dependent on mano, and mano is dependent on vinnana. It is impossible to kill or take away vinnana; however, we can alter all three states with efforts and by following the path of Buddha.

The Four Noble Truth

The Four Noble Truths or 'Char Arya Satya' can be called the essence of Buddha's teaching. These four truths are mysterious and often confusing for many. These four truths are dukkha or the truth of suffering, samudaya, or the origin of suffering, nirodha, meaning that dukkha can be ended, and magga or the path to end dukkha. In simpler terms, suffering exists in the world, it has a cause, it can be ended, and there is a way to bring about its end. While suffering is often considered negative by many people, in Buddhism, it is a pragmatic concept that looks at the world from a realistic point of view and tries to correct it. In Buddhism, pleasure is not a tabooed concept; however, it does consider it to be a fleeting and temporal concept. It believes that if a person shows an unquenchable thirst for pleasure, then it will only lead to unhappiness. Nothing is certain in life except illness, aging, and death.

The Four Noble Truth contains the summary of many other teachings of Buddha and thus forms the crux of his philosophy.

According to Buddha, dukkha is inevitable, and one of the only truths of life. Dukkha is often translated as pain, suffering, etc. It is a Pali word that means pain.

Dukkha is a significant philosophical concept in Buddhism. It is closely related to pain and suffering; however, it goes beyond them. It is also related to dissatisfaction, unfulfilled desires, etc., but ultimately, dukkha as a concept can have many meanings. The feeling of dissatisfaction, too, can arise from a variety of reasons, including impermanence, pain, vulnerability, etc.

Impermanence or anicca in Pali has a close connection to dukkha. It is often referred to in Buddha's teachings. It is impermanence that drove out Siddhartha out of his palace in search of truth and enlightenment. Impermanence in Buddhism can be anywhere between cosmic to microscopic. At the cosmic level, Buddha says that the universe is gigantic, and it is always evolving and breaking down in repetitive cycles right from the beginning of time and will continue to do so forever. On mortal levels, impermanence refers to the inescapable nature of mortality and how we are bound to sickness, aging, and death. Our body can die, it can disintegrate, and it can be destroyed as well.

Understanding of this impermanence allows us to understand the universality of dukkha. Buddha says that dukkha is omnipresent and is felt and experienced by everyone.

Karma

The concept of Karma is common in many Indian philosophical schools. It has also found a comfortable place in popular culture in the West. Many people think that karma means preordained fate; however, this is a myth. Karma is nothing but the good or bad deeds that people do during their lifetime. Karma is often translated as 'credit' in South East Asian nations. Good actions can either be genuinely positive actions such as charity, meditation, generosity, etc. or they can also be actions devoid of negativity. Bad actions are negative in nature. They include stealing, lying, killing, bringing unhappiness to others, etc. The weight of karma depends on many different things, they include: whether the action you did of repeated and done frequently, whether it was an intentional action, whether you regret the action, whether you did a bad action towards a person who had done a good action for you, whether the action was performed against an extraordinary person etc. Good actions beget good karma, while bad actions lead to bad karma. Along with these two, there is another form of karma, which is known as neutral karma. Neutral karma has no benefits or cons. It is gained from activities such as eating, breathing, sleeping, etc.

The Cycle of Rebirth

In Buddhism, the cycle of rebirth is controlled by karma. According to Buddhism, a person can be born in one of six different planes available. The people who did good actions get reborn in one of the three positive realms. The people who did mostly bad actions in their lifetime are sent to one of the remaining three, negative realm. The positive realms are named after demigods, gods, and human beings. The gods and demigods love the gratification; however, they can also be jealous. The realm of man or human beings is the topmost realm. It is the highest realm of rebirth. While this realm is not as attractive as the ones with demigod and gods, it is still safe and conflict-free. The three negative realms are animal realm, ghost realm, and hell itself.

The realm of man is also at the top because it allows people to devote their lives to the pursuit of nirvana once again. This is impossible in other realms. If the number and types of living things are to be taken into account, it is easy to say that getting a human birth is rare and should be celebrated.

Buddhism and Happiness

Buddha believed that the way of happiness begins by understanding the cause of suffering. Suffering forms a crucial part of Buddhism. No wonder many people reject Buddha as a pessimist. Thinking of Buddha as a pessimist is misguided and wrong. Buddha was concerned with suffering and pain, not because he liked them; it was because he wanted to understand them. As a doctor, Buddha looked at suffering clinically, and he wanted to treat it. The medicine that Buddha found for suffering was summarized in his teachings. However, like every other illness, the illness of suffering or dukkha can only be cured when the patient follows the advice of the doctor. If the path shown by Buddha is followed properly, you will be able to understand pain and suffering.

The treatment for suffering is a complex medicine. You need to practice mindful thoughts and actions daily. You need to concentrate on your feelings, emotions, and experience. One of the best ways to do this is by meditation. Many people think of meditation as a way of escaping or getting detached from the world. This is a myth; meditation is not an escapist's paradise; rather, it is a complex way of training the mind not to dwell on things, whether past or future. The present is far more important than the future or the past in Buddhism.

The way we act, live, and behave is a result of what we think. Our existence is firmly rooted in our thoughts. Our thoughts and actions can control our feelings and our fate, as well. For instance, if you speak or act negatively, you will feel pain.

As said earlier, suffering is a crucial concept in Buddhism, but happiness is the nucleus around which Buddhism revolves. Almost all the contemporaries of Buddha described him as 'ever-smiling.' Even the ancient and current portrayals of Buddha almost always depict him with a mysterious and mystique smile. It is not the smile of a celebrated man; neither is it the sign of a man indulged in hedonistic ways. Buddha's smile is far subtler because it comes from a deep understanding of the world. It comes from equanimity or the peace of mind and happiness.

Many people believe that happiness can only be begotten from materialistic pleasures. This belief has become even more prevalent in the current consumerist society. Buddhists, however, look for happiness in a very different place. In Buddhism, true happiness can be achieved with the help of knowledge and practice. While you may receive momentary pleasure from hedonistic activities, however momentary pleasure does not equal to true happiness. True happiness is equanimity or peace of mind. This peace of mind can only be achieved by detaching yourself from needs, desires, passions, and other factors that produce dukkha or suffering. If you can achieve such a mental state, then you become free and reach a state of transcendent happiness.

Buddha believed that mental dysfunction has its roots in mind. This is why Buddha encouraged his followers to seek 'tranquility' along with 'insight.' He believed that these mental qualities would lead his followers to nirvana. You will find more about this in the Eightfold Path. Ultimately Buddha believed that the right mindfulness, right efforts, and right concentration could lead everyone towards happiness.

In one of his sermons, Buddha compared the mind to a wild horse. In his Eightfold Path, Buddha asks his followers to practice the 'right effort.' In this, he advises them to clean their minds of unwholesome and negative thoughts. Once this cleansing is done, one can achieve true tranquility with the help of positive thinking. This is a continuous and ongoing effort that is accompanied with meditation and mindfulness. Let us have a brief look at mindfulness now.

Mindfulness

Mindfulness is considered to be one of the most important teachings of Buddha. It has had widespread influence and is now practiced by many non-Buddhists as well. It also finds an important place in modern psychotherapy, along with the popular culture. Buddha believed that right mindfulness was necessary for every aspect of our lives. This allows us to see things for what they really are. He wanted his followers to 'take things slow' and observe things. He encouraged them to develop a keen sense of attention, along with awareness. According to Buddha, the following are the four foundations of mindfulness.

- Contemplation of the body

- Contemplation of feelings

- Contemplation of states of mind

- Contemplation of phenomena

In simpler words, mindfulness is experiencing every little moment with openness and freshness. Buddha believed that with proper mindfulness, everyone could free themselves from cravings and passions.

Meditation

There are various different practices that come under the Buddhist concept of meditation. Right Concentration holds a special place in Buddhism. It is one of the major practices, which form the basis of many other, far more complex meditations, and practices.

According to Shakyamuni Buddha, Deep Meditation has four stages of concentration. These stages are as follows:

- First Stage: In the first stage, the mind slowly starts becoming pure and calm. All negativity is slowly drained from the mind.

- Second Stage: In the second stage, all activities of the mind and mental hindrances disappear. A feeling of bliss fills the mind.

- Third Stage: In this stage, the mind slowly starts becoming empty. The feeling of bliss disappears, leaving behind a faint sense of happiness.

- Fourth Stage: This is the last stage of concentration in deep meditation. In this stage, the mind truly becomes empty, and even the fleeting sense of bliss disappears. A feeling of total peace and emptiness descends on your mind. Buddha called this state a state of deep happiness.

Compassion

Buddha is well known around the world for his compassion and love. He preached the truth, but he also saw compassion because he believed that true happiness could only be gained when others are happy as well. Buddha not only preached this but also adhered to it strictly, in life as well as death. It is believed that Buddha achieved nirvana just because he wanted to teach the way of transcendence to others. It is also said that one of Buddha's followers poisoned him accidentally. Buddha did not get angry with this follower; rather, he said that the meal was one of the two most blessed meals that he had ever had in his life. The first blessed meal was the meal that he consumed to break his fast under the Bodhi tree, which showed him the way to nirvana, and the second, poisoned meal, which would lead him to the way of Mahanirvana.

Ultimately, the path to attain a deeper form of happiness is difficult because you need to face the fact that life is considered to be full of dukkha in Buddhism. Buddhism is closely associated with the mind and its various conditions, including emotions, feelings, etc. It believes that only by understanding the mind properly, one can achieve true happiness.

Buddhism in the Modern World

Buddhism is rapidly becoming one of the most prominent and popular faiths around the world. There are numerous Buddhist centers and shrines in European nations, South America, Africa, North America, Australia, etc. Buddhism has spread around not only in the western capitalist societies but also in socialist nations. Even in small nations like Poland, there are more than five thousand Buddhist practitioners. Why is it so that a thousands years old religion is suddenly gaining such widespread attention all over?

The appeal of Buddhism can be traced to its rational and scientific attitude. In Buddhism, you are taught to critic things. As Buddha said, "Never believe in anything that I preach just because you respect me, go ahead and test it, analyze it as if you were shopping for gold." This non-dogmatic approach is quite compatible with the psyche of the modern people.

Many current prominent leaders of various Buddhist schools, such as the Dalai Lama and others, have been invited to talk and discuss matters of great importance with eminent scientists. They have discussed the nature and essence of reality, along with many other things. Buddha preached that all our sufferings and problems are a result of not understanding the true nature of reality. This confusion leads to pain. If people had an awareness of who we are and why we are in this world etc. it would not create problems and confusion. Thus Buddha taught his followers to cultivate a questioning, inquisitive, curious nature. Many Buddhist leaders have proclaimed that if scientists prove that something that Buddha preached or followed is a superstition or incorrect, they would gladly drop it from their practice and instead take up the new scientific proof and preach it. This kind of approach is rarely seen in other religions, which makes Buddhism attractive.

The all-accepting and curious nature of Buddhism is not a new thing. Teachers and monks adapted Buddhism to the culture of each new society they visited, which facilitated its spread. Similarly, modern teachers are more than ready to assimilate, adapt, and adapt to new things. Ultimately, rationality is a crucial point in Buddhism.

Buddha taught many different methods of preaching, teaching, and learning because he had many different students who came from many different cultural, social, economic, and otherwise backgrounds. He knew that people would change even more in the future, and only one form or method of teaching would work. For example, we love eating different types of foods and wearing different types of clothes. Instead, imagine if we had only one type of food available, we would soon get tired of it. Similarly, it is possible this one type of food may or may not appeal to everyone. This is why Buddha taught many different methods according to the wide spectrum of tastes of people. Ultimately the objective of Buddhism is overcoming problems with our efforts and realizing our potential.

Buddhism is one of the few, or perhaps the only religion in the world that emphasizes a rational approach, critical thinking, and scientific attitude, and aptitude. Buddha believed that a person could not be truly wise until he or she develops logic and rationality. Buddhism presents a clear picture of how various experiences in life happen and how a person should deal with them in a way that will not cause anyone pain. Buddhism teaches followers to question things. It tells them that they should never accept a thing on its face value before thinking about it. It strictly promotes critical thinking and vehemently opposes blind faith. Nothing is to be considered sacred until you yourself test it out. If the results positive, only then a person is allowed to believe it.

Nowadays, consumers have become smart, and they do not purchase anything until they examine it properly. For instance, nobody likes to buy a car without test-driving it. Similarly, you should never accept something without testing it. This includes the philosophy of life and religion, as well. Do not make a life-changing choice without check whether it would suit your lifestyle or not. This is why a lot of people in the 21st century are moving on to Buddhism. As said earlier, in Buddhism, scientific inquiry is a must. This sits well with modern times- a fact that has made Buddhism so popular all around the world.

In certain Western nations such as Switzerland and the USA, psychology is considered to be a significant subject. Many Buddhist teachers present Buddhism through the lens of psychology in these nations. In nations that focus more on devotion and preaching, such as Latin America and Southern Europe, the teachers preach a devotional version of Buddhism. People who love chanting mantras really like the devotional method of preaching. In the Northern European nations, however, the teachers preach in a far more intelligent way.

Thus the style of preaching changes according to the nature of people and cultural demands.

Many nations in Eastern Europe live in abject poverty and violence. Such people find the presence of Buddha soothing in their lives. They believe that Buddhism can fill the empty space in their lives. Buddhism teaches people that working hard and making efforts can really help. It also makes people enthusiastic and appreciative of their lives ad work.

Thus Buddhism can adapt easily to the mentality and culture of people wherever it goes. Yet, it never forgoes the teachings of Buddha. The principles are never changed — only the approach of presenting them changes.

Chapter Four: Buddhism - Ancient Techniques in the Modern World

Buddhism is one of the oldest religions in the world, and it has undergone a lot of changes and evolution throughout this time. One of the most prominent things about Buddhism is that it's highly adaptive. It's flexible, and thus, it changed and adjusted itself according to the place and time. This is why there are so many different versions of Buddhism currently being practiced in the world. While these branches of Buddhism are different, most of their core principles remain the same. These principles are ancient, yet they are still relevant to modern times. In this chapter, let us have a look at these principles and ancient techniques of Buddhism.

The Noble Eightfold Path

The Noble Eight-fold Path consists of the following eight parts:

- Samma Ditthi: Right understanding and vision
- Samma Sankappa: Right thoughts and ideas
- Samma Vaca: Right speech
- Samma Kammanta: Right actions
- Samma Ajiva: Right livelihood
- Samma Vayama: Right efforts
- Samma Sati: Right mindfulness
- Samma Samadhi: Right concentration

Almost all of Buddha's teachings are related to the Eight-fold Path in some way. He often explained the path in many different words and different ways according to the need of his followers. While the methods may have been different, but the essence of those many thousand discourses scattered in the Buddhist scriptures is found in the noble eightfold path.

The eight-fold path is to follow as per the capacity of the practitioner. It is possible that you may not be able to follow certain parts of the path at first; however, with constant efforts, you will be successful in your endeavor. You do not need to follow the eight-fold path sequentially; instead, you can do it according to your capacity.

The eight-fold path is essential as it promotes and perfects the three important concepts of the Buddhist discipline. These three concepts are

- Sila or Ethical conduct

- Samadhi or Mental discipline

- Panna or Wisdom

Let us have a close look at all the eight divisions of the eight-fold path and their categories one by one.

Ethical Conduct (Sila)

Sila or ethical conduct is based on the concept of universal compassion and love. In this love, every living being is included. Many scholars fail to focus on this concept and often discuss Buddhism and the teachings of Buddha in a dry and academic manner. It should be noted that Buddha taught people because he believed in 'for the good of all, for the happiness of all, because of compassion for the world.'

As per the Buddhist doctrine, a person can be perfect only when he or she posses a balanced nature with Karuna (compassion) on one side and Panna (wisdom) on the other side. Karuna or compassion stands for charity, love, tolerance, kindness, and all such noble qualities related to feelings and emotions. These qualities are traditionally associated with the heart. Panna or wisdom stands for all intellectual and mental qualities. Thus, Buddhism preaches a total balance of the heart and the brain. If anyone of these two is neglected, then the person is imperfect. For instance, if you possess only the qualities of the heart, you will become a kindhearted fool. Similarly, if you develop only the intellectual qualities, then you will become a stonehearted person who will only care for his own selfish interests. It is thus necessary to develop both these sides equally. Buddha believed that wisdom and compassion are inseparable and should stay like that.

Let us now have a look at the parts of the Eight-fold path that come under the Sila section.

Right Speech

Right speech or sometimes translated as right words includes abstaining from lying, slander, backbiting, etc. In the right speech, people are advised to avoid using language that may cause enmity, hatred, disunity, and disharmony among people. You should not be rude, harsh, malicious, and impolite. You should not abuse others and should avoid gossiping and indulging in useless chatter. All these forms of speech are incorrect and should be avoided. When you successfully abstain from these, you will only speak the truth in a simple, pleasant, gentle, and benevolent way. You will only speak things that you find useful or meaningful. You should always speak carefully with ample consideration of the place, time, and situation. Buddha believed that if you do not have anything good or useful to say, then you should keep your silence. Nothing is nobler than silence.

Right Action

The right action governs our conduct. It promotes honorable, moral, and peaceful conduct. Under this part, you are not allowed to steal, destroy life, be dishonest, or have illegitimate sexual relations. You are supposed to help people live an honorable and pleasant life.

Right Livelihood

Right livelihood means that you should not obtain your livelihood from illegal activities. It also means that you should indulge in trades that can cause others harm. This includes selling poisons and intoxicating chemicals such as alcohol, trading in weapons, killing animals, etc. Cheating is strictly banned in Buddhism. Buddha believed that everyone should earn their livelihood in an honorable way. If your means of livelihood are harming others, then it is recommended to introspect and change your job. Buddhism is strongly opposed to war and believes that trading weapons are an unjust and evil way to earn money.

Thus these three factors constitute Sila. Buddha wanted life to be harmonious and happy for everyone. He believed that such a life could only be achieved with proper moral conduct, as advised in this section. You cannot achieve spiritual bliss until your moral base is strong.

Mental Discipline (Samadhi)

The next section is Samadhi or mental discipline. In this section, three more factors of the eightfold path are included.

They are the right effort, right mindfulness, and right concentration. Let us have a look at them one by one.

Right Effort

According to Buddha, you should use your energy to prevent evil and do good. He believed that with efforts, one can get rid of unwholesome thoughts, evil ideas and can destroy them forever. The right effort also includes developing once positive ideas and a wholesome state of mind.

Right Mindfulness

In this, one needs to be aware and attentive about the Kaya, Vedana, Citta, and Dhamma. Kaya means the activities of the body, vedana stands for feelings, citta means the activities of the mind, and Dhamma means conceptions, thoughts, etc.

Mindfulness is often achieved with the help of many different breathing exercises. One such exercise is the anapanasati or concentrating on breathing. There are many other ways of being mindful such as many different forms of mediation etc.

One needs to pay close attention to the feelings and sensations that they feel. These sensations can be pleasant, unpleasant, or even neutral. All these are interconnected, and they rise and disappear within them like flames. You should try to keep your mind free of everything. You should be aware whether your mind is deluded or not, whether it has hatred or not, whether it is lustful or not, whether it is concentrated or distracted etc. Paying close attention to your feelings, and being aware of them is essential in Buddhism.

One should understand how things, thoughts, and ideas appear and disappear. People should also understand the nature of these objects.

You will find more about mindfulness later in the book.

Right Concentration (Dhyana)

The last factor that comes under mental discipline is the right concentration. Right concentration is essential because it leads to Dhyana or trance. In the first stage of Dhyana, all ill feelings such as worry, languor, lust, doubt, and restlessness are destroyed. Only happiness and joy remains. In the second stage, all intellectual activities such as thoughts and ideas are suppressed, and only tranquility remains. In the third stage of Dhyana, the active feeling of happiness disappears; however, the overall aura of peace remains. In the final stage, the whole mind becomes empty, and even the sensation of happiness disappears. The mind becomes totally blank and, the only equanimity remains.

Thus the mind is disciplined and trained carefully through right effort, right mindfulness, and right concentration.

Wisdom

The third section includes the remaining two parts of the eight-fold path, which are the right thought and right understanding.

Right Thought

The idea of right thought encompasses selfless renunciation and detachment. In this, you are supposed to extend thoughts of peace, love, tranquility, and non-violence towards all living beings. A noteworthy thing here is that the concept of love and non-violence is grouped under the banner of wisdom. This proves that Buddha believed that a person could not be truly wise until he or she posses these noble qualities. If a person has selfish desires, or his or her mind is full of violence, hatred, etc. then he or she is not wise.

Right Understanding

Right understanding means understanding and analyzing things as they are. The Four Noble Truths explain the reality of everything; thus, the right understanding means understanding the noble truths. Understanding the noble truth allows you to understand the Ultimate Reality. According to Buddhist principles, there are two kinds of understandings. One is our generic understanding related to memory, knowledge, etc. This kind of understanding is known as anubodha, which means knowing accordingly. This kind of understanding is not deep. The second type of understanding is called pativedha or seeing a thing in its true nature without any label or name. This is a real and deep understanding. This kind of understanding can only be achieved with the help of meditation and mindfulness.

From the above discussion of the Noble Eight-fold Path, it is clear that the way is an immaculate way of attaining nirvana. It is an adaptive path that can change according to the needs and requirements of the individual. It teaches the followers to become self-disciplined not only physically but also mentally, socially, and verbally. It focuses on the purification and development of the follower without involving any prayers, ceremonies, or even worship. It is truly secular in nature and has nothing to do with the popular notions of 'religion.' It is a path that can be followed by anyone to achieve true freedom, complete peace, and total spiritual, intellectual, and moral perfection.

The Three Jewels of Buddhism

The Three Jewels of Buddhism, also known as the Triratna, Three Gems,

Three Diamonds, etc. of Buddhism, can be considered to be the foundation of all forms and schools of Buddhism. These three are the core of Buddhism, and the follower is supposed to seek refuge in them. These three are Buddha, Dhamma, and Sangha. In this section, let us have a look at all these three Jewels one by one.

Buddha

Buddha is the first jewel of Buddhism. The word Buddha means 'one who is enlightened or one who is Awake.' While the word Buddha is often associated with Shakyamuni Buddha or the historical Buddha, in Triratna, it achieves a far more significant status. Here the word means everyone who has become enlightened and has achieved his or her full potential. These Buddhas are supposed to be the teachers of everyone. Them being teachers is as important as them being enlightened.

Nirvana, freedom from suffering, liberation, salvation, etc. everything comes only when you understand your own reality. Shakyamuni Buddha believed that no one could help you achieve nirvana; only your own efforts can help you do so. He preached that no magical way of enlightenment exists. It is not a secret, nor is it a gimmick. It won't come through meditation either. You need to incorporate a lot of things to reach enlightenment.

Buddha then stands for a teacher who can guide us and show us the path to enlightenment. Teaching should not be dogmatic. A teacher should provide his or her student's tools through which they can learn, study, and develop themselves.

It is, therefore, the historical Buddha believes that all followers should take refuge in Buddha. This forms the first line of the Trisharan (The Three Refuge): Buddham Sharanam Gacchami, which means I take refuge in Buddha. The nature of Buddha as a concept is secular. It does not mean that you need to take refuge in a religious teacher or preacher; in Buddhism, a Buddha or a teacher can be anyone, including your schoolteacher as well.

Dhamma

The second jewel is Dhamma or Dharma. Dhamma has a much different meaning. The highest meaning of Dhamma means the reality that helps us stay in a state of bliss. Dhamma is also our reality that we strive hard to understand completely. Dhamma also incorporates all the methods of teachings present in arts and science that can help up to become aware of our reality.

The qualities that we develop, the ethics that we follow, the practices that we undertake, which can lead us to freedom, all come under the concept of Dhamma. This is why some people consider Dhamma to be synonymous with religion. In Vedic Brahmanism, Dhamma, aka Dharma, also stands for duty and routines; however, Buddha freed the concept from these restraints. In Buddhism, Dhamma is the journey towards freedom.

When a follower is asked to take refuge in Dhamma, he or she is asked to take refuge in reality itself. Taking refuge in anything that is unreal is insecure, as it is temporary. Reality is not created by anyone, and thus, it lasts. Thus it can provide you refuge.

It is, therefore, Buddha believed that all followers should take refuge in Dhamma. This forms the second line of the Trisharan: Dhammam Sharanam Gacchami, which means I take refuge in Dhamma.

Sangha

The third jewel of Buddhism is Sangha or the community. Community includes everyone who seeks refuge in the three jewels and who are trying to achieve freedom. All such people in Sangha are evolving continuously and are walking on the path towards becoming Buddha. Sangha includes every Buddhist in this world.

This forms the last line of the Trisharan: Sangham Sharanam Gacchami, which means I take refuge in Sangha.

Thus the complete Trisharan is as follows:

Buddham Sharanam Gacchami

Dhammam Sharanam Gacchami

Sangham Sharanam Gacchami

All Buddhists throughout the world say this either in Pali or in their native language. Taking refuge in Buddha, Dhamma, and Sangha has multiple meanings. Taking refuge is not only a pious and meditative act; rather, it is also an act that restores your faith and energy. It allows you to have much-needed rest and serenity. Thus, the Three Jewels form the core of Buddhism.

Five Precepts

The five precepts (or Pancasila in Pali) are the five rules of training in Buddhism philosophy and practice. It is an essential system of morality that Buddhists are supposed to follow. This code consists of various ethical practices that all practitioners of Buddhism must adhere to. The precepts are rather simple and mostly deal with moral and ethical practices such as not lying, not killing living organisms, not stealing, not indulging in sexual misconduct, and avoiding intoxication. According to Buddhist practice, these five precepts are meant to help people follow the path of enlightenment. Certain Mahayana scholars refer to them as 'sravakayana' precepts, which are different from the 'bodhisattva precepts.' The five precepts are crucial to the Buddhism philosophy, and monks, as well as common people, are supposed to follow them. Many people compare these precepts with the ten commandments of Abrahamic religions and sometimes with the codes of conduct of Confucianism. In modern times many scholars believe that the precepts complement the concept of human rights and are universal in nature.

The Five Precepts are as follows:

Panatipata veramani sikkhapadam samadiyami!

(I receive the training-precept to stay away from killing living/breathing beings.)

Adinnadana veramani sikkhapadam samadiyami!

(I receive the training-precept to stay away from taking what is not mine or snatching what is not given.)

Kamesumicchacara veramani sikkhapadam samadiyami!

(I receive the training-precept to stay away from sexual misconduct.)

Musavada veramani sikkhapadam samadiyami!

(I receive the training-precept to stay away from false speech.)

Suramerayamajjapamadatthana veramani sikkhapadam samadiyami!

(I receive the training-precept to stay away from intoxicating products and substances.)

These are often recited in the presence of monks along with the Trisharan.

The five precepts were common to the overall religious atmosphere in the time of Buddha; however, Buddha found them important and thoroughly focused on them. The importance of the five precepts kept on increasing day by day, which is observed in the Buddhist scriptures. Ultimately, the five precepts became one of the main conditions of becoming a Buddhist. The nature of the five precepts changed with time and according to regions. For instance, in China and similar nations, the five precepts were developed into a sort of initiation ceremony, which a new follower must undergo to become a Buddhist truly. This was because, in China and similar regions, Buddhism had to compete with other religions. In other nations such as Thailand, where Buddhism had virtually no competition, no ceremonial or ritualistic aspect got attached to the five precepts. In such nations, people were thought to be born Buddhists naturally.

It is necessary to not only undertake the five precepts but uphold them as well. The Pali Canon teaches practitioners to compare themselves with others before hurting them. Buddhists are taught to believe in karma and compassion. These two factors form the basis of the precepts. Reciting and undertaking the precepts is a common Buddhist practice that is often done in monasteries, temples, and homes. In many Buddhist sects, it is also used in various ceremonies such as weddings where the Pancasila assumes the position of marital vows. People tend to uphold the precepts out of devotion towards Buddha and also the fear of bad rebirth.

These are often recited in the presence of monks along with the Trisharan. All the above sentences are loaded with meaning, and thus, they are often interpreted in various ways according to the need and requirements of the time, law, and place. For instance, the first precepts talk about abstaining from killing any breathing and or living being. Many scholars believe that this precept prohibits capital punishment along with suicide, euthanasia, and sometimes abortion. However, many Buddhist nations still use the death penalty in modern times. Buddhists generally believe in non-violence, which is often interpreted as opposing violence; however, many scholars disagree with this and believe that defense is not violence.

The second precept deals with theft. No kind of stealing is allowed in Buddhism. This includes physical objects and mental ideas, as well.

The third precept deals with adultery and sexual misconduct. Scholars believe that this stands for responsible sexual activities and commitment.

The fourth precept refers to dishonest speech. This includes malicious speech, gossip, lying, slander, harsh speech, etc.

The fifth precept advises practitioners to avoid intoxication. Intoxication is a loaded word and can refer to many things such as alcohol, drugs, etc. Almost all Buddhist sects and texts are against alcohol. The attitude towards smoking keeps on changing quite often, but in modern times, it is generally tolerated (for common people only).

In the West, the five precepts are considered to be major by many Buddhist organizations. Many meditations and mindfulness trainers incorporate the five precepts in their sessions, as well.

Buddhism: Stress and Anxiety

Stress is one of the most searched and talked about things nowadays. It is difficult to find a person who is not stressed today. Everyone is either anxious about something or worried about another. While it is true the world and life have become more stressful now, stress itself is not a new thing; people have felt and have tried to deal with stress since the beginning of time. In Buddhism, stress and getting rid of it is an important thing because stress often creates hurdles in the path of enlightenment. The question of stress and suffering is the nucleus of Buddhism. It was stress and suffering that made prince Siddhartha quite his pleasant life and went away in search of peace. Thus, Buddha, his teachings, and his followers have examined stress on many different levels and have provided us with many different perspectives as well.

The Experience of Stress

Stress is an extremely uncomfortable feeling that creates unpleasant sensations. Stress is often experienced in the form of anxiety and pretty. Some people also feel a claustrophobic sensation due to stress. Stress feels like a sea of pain in which you drown continuously without dying. You may feel overwhelmed by everything, and even the littlest thing can blow your fuse. Stress attacks your mind from all sides and corners it. If you are stressed, even the simplest activity such as brushing your teeth may seem like a Herculean task. A stressed person feels entrapped.

Stress affects our bodies and minds physically too. Our body gets tighter; some people also experience pain in muscles. We get edgy and afraid. Even the slightest irritation can lead to an uncontrollable fit of anger.

Many times when we are stressed, we try to find someone whom we can blame. We think that only some external objects can cause these feelings, and if we get rid of the object, everything will go back to normal. In rare cases, there might be a physical object, which you can and should remove immediately. However, stress is often due to internal situations and causes which cannot be discarded immediately.

The Buddhist tradition considers stress to be a part of life. It understands the reality of stress and how discomforting it is. It is acknowledged in the first noble truth itself, which makes it so difficult to accept. We often think that a little tweak and change in lifestyle will help us get rid of stress. For instance, you may think if you were wealthier, smarter, prettier, etc. all your problems would be solved automatically. But this never happens, they are not realistic, and you are not accepting your reality. It is unrealistic to desire for a stress-free life, which is why Buddhism focuses on helping you make sense of stress and learn how to deal with it.

Stress is often exaggerated by your mind, especially when it is not calm and is unbalanced. It is also exaggerated when your mind is preoccupied with things. Mindfulness and compassion can help you clear your mind and allow you to look at stress in an objective way. Remember, it is unrealistic to expect a stress-free life; you need to accept its reality. Instead of viewing it as an unbeatable foe, look at stress as a puzzle that can be solved with the right tools and moves.

Chapter Five: Meditation, Yoga, and Buddhism

Meditation and yoga have become quite popular throughout the world in recent times. Many people confuse them for the same thing; however, there are many differences between them. In this chapter, let us have a close look at meditation and yoga.

Meditation

There are many different forms of meditation that are advised in Buddhism, but before moving on to them, let us have a look at some questions related to meditation and Buddhism.

What is Meditation?

There are many different types and interpretations of meditation. Buddhist meditation, for instance, is the practice of exercising your mind. Every meditation in Buddhism starts with various practices that help you to become calm and concentrate on your mind only. Once you are calm and focused, you can start to investigate the truth of reality and develop insight as well.

One of the most common forms of meditation in Buddhism is breath meditation. In this form, you are supposed to concentrate on your breathing. You find the instructions for this form of meditation later in this section. As Buddhism is a family of sects, schools, and practices, different branches and sub-branches of Buddhism have different instructions and interpretations of mediation. Vipassana, a popular form of meditation, is supposed to have been taught by Shakyamuni Buddha himself. The Zazen, a form of mediation from the Zen school, is thought to be a stripped-down version of the above-mentioned breathing practice.

Why Meditate?

There are many different reasons why you should meditate. Every person has his or her own reason why they should meditate. The 17th Karmapa, a Tibetan Buddhist teacher, says that meditation can help us realize that we are full of compassion and wisdom. Meditation can also calm and relax your body and mind. But this calm and serenity are accompanied by the profound realization and a strange awareness of our existence. It can help you to cut through the entire chase, discard problems, errors, and misconceptions and instead form a compassionate and loving relationship with yourself.

Some people also meditate to cultivate positive traits. For instance, meditation can help you become courageous and steadfast. It can also increase your attention span and make you more focused. It also has positive results in your relationship. Many people have proclaimed that mediation made them more resilient.

While all the above-mentioned things are perfectly valid reasons for meditation, ultimately, Buddha preached mediation because he believed it to be a crucial tool to achieve nirvana.

What Challenges Will I Face While Meditating?

While there are no significant challenges or problems associated with meditation as such, people may still feel bad about certain things. For instance, many people believe that they can be either good or bad at meditation. This is false for meditation is as simple as breathing.

Many people are also confused about the timing and period of mediation. Buddhists believe that any time you spend meditating, whether short or long, is ultimately beneficial. Start with whatever feels comfortable and slowly increase the duration. Once you form the habit, you will find meditating relaxing and easy to do.

Some people also complain of physical discomfort while meditating. This is a common problem, and even the most experienced practitioners feel discomfort from time to time. With time the physical discomfort will go away. You can also use tools such as pillows to make yourself more comfortable.

Some forms of Meditation

Buddha believed that we should be able to meditate anywhere and in any position. Buddhist texts talk of standing meditation, sitting meditation, walking meditation, and lying down meditation as well. Ideally, you should be able to meditate while doing almost anything. Let us have a look at some of the most popular forms of meditation in this section.

Breath Meditation

Breath meditation is the simplest form of meditation, which makes it so popular. It is also considered to the base of many other forms of meditation.

Instructions

- If you have a meditation room, then move on to the second step, if you don't have one then find a calm and peaceful corner in your house and spread your yoga mat there.

- Sit down, your legs should be crossed, and feet should be flat on the floor. You can use a pillow or meditation cushion to support yourself.

- Choose a sitting posture. For instance, you can put your hands on your thighs (palm down). Sit upright and keep your posture straight. You should be dignified yet relaxed.

- Start focusing on your breath. Keep the attention light and slowly start dissolving in the space around you.

- Keep close attention to the thoughts that may arise while focusing on breathing. If you ever think that your attention has gone awry, just return to the breath slowly. This happens even with the most senior and experienced practitioners, so don't judge yourself for it.

- After the end of the stipulated time, slowly come out of your meditative state and relax. Try to keep the aura and sense of calm and openness stable — all it to remain present throughout the day.

Shamatha

Shamatha is a popular Buddhist practice that focuses on clarity of thought, calmness, and equanimity. It is also known as the Buddhist practice of mindfulness. The cultivation of the above-mentioned qualities can help you achieve deep inner peace. This practice is often combined with Vipassana practices. This combination can help you become spiritually away and insightful. Anyone can practice this meditation.

Instructions

- Sit in a meditation posture. You should be comfortable, and your knees and back should not hurt.

- Slowly pay attention to your breathing, however, only focus on breathing out. You should focus on one breath at a time.

- Acknowledge all the thoughts that come to your mind but don't engage with them. Let them float away gently. If you ever get confused or distracted, don't worry and just go back to breathing. This is also known as 'touch and go.' Whenever a thought arises, do not kill or ignore it, just let it float away.

Metta

Another popular method of Buddhist meditation is Metta. It is also known as kindness meditation. Many different forms of this meditation exist as well, but all of them begin with simple breathing exercises to calm your mind. Your mind should be receptive and settled else you won't be able to meditate properly.

Instructions

- In one of the most popular forms of this meditation, you are supposed to direct your wishes of kindness and wellbeing towards yourself.

- Slowly direct these wishes towards people that you love.

- After this, you are supposed to direct these wishes towards people about whom you are neutral.

- Later direct these wishes towards people that you despise.

- You are supposed to direct your feelings of love and compassion towards everyone equally. You may be angry with someone or may dislike them, but you still should be full of compassion for them. The feeling of love will dull the feeling of enmity. You will start feeling real compassion for the person, and your mind will be full of purity and devoid of any negativity. This mediation thus concentrates on benevolence and compassion.

Some people also chant mantras and holy prayers while performing this meditation. Things like 'May everyone is happy and calm.' 'May everyone achieve their goals of love.' etc. can be chanted to help you perform this meditation.

Once the period of metta practice is done, practitioners sit and experience the feeling of peace and tranquility for a while.

Contemplative Meditation

Another popular form of Buddhist meditation is contemplative meditation. In this, practitioners are asked to reflect on themselves in a contemplative and highly focused manner. One of the best-known forms of this meditation is 'The Four Thoughts the Transform Mind.' In this method, you are supposed to sit down and contemplate instead of wasting time on social media and other such useless activities. Let us have a look at these four thoughts:

- I possess the ability to devote my energy towards developing compassion, wisdom, and power to help others. I believe that this opportunity is precious because not all can have it. I vow to use it well and not waste it.

- I understand that life is a cycle of continuous change, and my golden opportunity may disappear. I have no time to waste.

- Everything that exists in this world exists for a reason. Every action that we commit has some sort of consequences. This is the truth of interdependence, and often our action may do a lot more harm or help than what we imagine.

- Ultimately we will be separated from the materialistic objects of this world. Everything that we loved and cherished will be lost forever. It is therefore recommended to focus our energy on being beneficial to society and develop the qualities of compassion, wisdom, and spirituality.

Guided Buddhist Meditation

Do you want to start Buddhist meditation, but don't know how? Are you confused about certain things that are causing problems with your practice? Then you should contact a Buddhist teacher and check whether they have guided meditation programs. Many institutes have specially designed meditation courses that are taught by experienced professionals.

If you do not have a meditation institute, you can also join a meditation class. This is a brilliant way of interacting with people and enjoying the benefits of being in a sangha.

Buddhism and Yoga

Yoga and Buddhism are two ancient Indian practices that have taken over the West. They have to lead to a revolution of physical as well as mental fitness. In the West, many people believe that Yoga and Buddhism are the same or are at least similar. While Buddhism and yoga both arose as sister traditions and have significant similarities, there are also a lot of differences in them that make them two distinct philosophies and practices. Yoga and Buddhism are both schools of Indian philosophy; however, they represent two opposite groups of the hermeneutics. Indian philosophy is divided into two groups called the Orthodox group and the heterodox group. The schools of philosophy that come under the orthodox group accept the Vedas while the heterodox do not accept it. The list of these schools is as follows:

Orthodox Schools: Vedanta, Mimamsa, Yoga, Samkhya, Vaishesika, and NyayaTrisharan

Heterodox Schools: Carvaka, Jain, Buddhism

As it is clear from above that Yoga and Buddhism fall in the opposite groups. Yoga believes and accepts the supremacy of Vedas (Hindu scriptures), while Buddhism and teachings of Buddha do not accept their supremacy. Buddha abhorred Vedic rituals and practices. Yoga believes in God, whereas traditional Buddhism either denies the existence of God or neither accepts it neither denies it.

In the West, the form of yoga that is prevalent is just one small part of the philosophy. The asanas or postures and the modern forms of yoga such as hatha yoga, Iyengar yoga, Ashtanga yoga, etc. all emphasize postures only and do not pay any attention to the philosophy. Such practices can be combined with Buddhism. Some of the benefits that regular asanas can have on Buddhism are:

Regular asana practice makes our mind and body sharp. It also helps us become disciplined, which is a big plus for people who find meditation difficult due to a lack of focus.

Asana practice makes our body flexible and strong. This allows a practitioner to sit and meditate for a long period. Asana practice can also help our posture.

Asana practice can also increase attention span and help people control their breathing.

Philosophically, Buddhism, and yoga share certain ideas; however, there are significant differences as well. Let us have a look at some of the similarities and differences in philosophies of yoga and Buddhism.

Similarities

- Both are ancient schools of philosophy from India.

- Both accept rebirth and karma.

- Both believe that we do not understand the reality, and it is distorted.

- Both believe that these distorted views cause problems such as attachment, desire, and anger.

- Both believe that these problems can be overcome by understanding the truth of reality.

- For preparing our minds to understand the truth, we need to concentrate and focus on the help of a code of conduct, ethics, and discipline.

- With ample training of the mind, a person can achieve nirvana/moksha.

All the above ideas are similar to each other; however, there exist many minor and major differences in the above concepts as well. For instance, moksha and nirvana may seem to be the same concept, but they are not.

Let us have a look at the major differences between these two philosophies.

Differences

- In yoga, the reality is considered to be 'Maya' or a non-existent illusion. In Buddhism, reality exists; however, our perception of reality is unrealistic, irrational, and often problematic.

- Yoga is a theistic practice where the creator Brahma is acknowledged, unlike Buddhism.

- In yoga, the final stage of liberation is the union of soul and Brahma. In Buddhism, mastering our own mind and getting rid of the negativity is the final stage. It does not involve any divine interception.

- While nonviolence, i.e., ahimsa, is practiced and promoted in both, yogis choose a more ascetic way while Buddhists follow the middle path. They are neither hedonistic nor ascetic.

Thus, incorporating the physical aspect of yoga in your daily Buddhist life is fine; however, you should avoid mixing the philosophical aspects as it may cause confusion.

Making Space in your Home for Meditation

Having a special room or corner in your home for meditation and mindfulness activities is recommended. The aura of the room will become positive. You will always feel optimistic when you will enter the room and will forget all your stress and problems for a while. It will not only recharge your mind but will also recharge your body.

There are no specific rules that you should follow while creating a meditation room/corner, but there are certain considerations that, if taken, can make your room the best place in your house. In this section, let us look at some tips that can help you transform a simple room into a paradise of peace.

1) Choose the corner/room

Your meditation room is supposed to make you feel tranquil and happy, so it is necessary to choose a room that has no negative memories attached to it. You should be able to walk into the room with a smile. It also needs to be quiet and away from noise and traffic. Your meditation room should get ample natural light. Avoid using too many artificial light sources. If you prefer dark while meditating, install ambient lights that will make the room serene while being dark.

If you do not like restricting yourself to rooms while meditating, you can also choose a corner in your yard and adjust it accordingly.

2) De-clutter

Once you have chosen your room, you should clean it thoroughly. An unclean atmosphere can get reflected in your meditation. If your room is cluttered, de-clutter it and throw away or donate anything that you do not need. Many people try and fail to meditate in their offices, as offices are too cluttered.

Keep your mediation room as simple as possible. If possible, just keep a few posters, a couple of yoga mats, rugs, a small table, and tools necessary for meditation.

3) A Green Touch

Plants and trees are the best gifts that nature has bestowed upon the earth. Add some natural elements to your meditation room. It will make it more beautiful and peaceful. Meditation deals with connecting your mind (and body) with your atmosphere and nature.

To add a touch of nature to your meditation room, you can add simple flowers, a couple of live plants, seashells, water fountains, etc. Plants that produce fragrant flowers such as jasmine are best for meditation.

4) Ambient Music

While music is often not a part of meditation, some people find it soothing and calming and allows them to meditate in a better way. Ambient music can especially helpful for people who live in noisy areas.

There many music choices, lists, and suggestions especially made for meditation available online. It is recommended to choose music without lyrics. Classical music is a great choice; however, you can also choose ambient sounds such as nature sounds, the sound of the sea, etc. Instead of making a playlist of sound, use a loop.

5) Aromatherapy

Meditation works not only on the mind but also on your overall body and senses. You can introduce pleasant and calming scents in your meditation room. These include chamomile, lavender, peppermint, natural jasmine, etc. You use essential oils, candles, frankincense, and similar products to create these smells.

6) Make it personal

If you are the only one who is going to use the mediation room, try to personalize it. If there are certain things that help you calm down, add them to your room. This may include statues of Buddha, some healing stones, bells, plants, chimes, crystals, or basically any other object that you love. But remember, do not overcrowd your room as it will distract you from your meditation.

7) Fresh Atmosphere

Along with aromatherapy, your room should have a continuous source of fresh air. Fresh air is essential for the health of your mind, body, and soul. It will keep you refreshed and active. If you normally meditate outside, then getting fresh air will not be difficult for you, however, if you meditate indoors, then select a room that is well ventilated. If your room does not have a fan, invest in a good quality 'silent' fan along with an air purifier. This will keep your room breezy and well ventilated.

8) Choosing a paint palette

The color of your room can affect your meditation, as well. Check out articles on color theory and how color affects your mood to know more about this. It is recommended to choose a color palette that matches the mood that you plan to achieve. Many people prefer pastels, while others believe that dark shades are more soothing- the choice is subjective to your needs and tastes.

9) Ambient Lights

Natural light, as said earlier, is best for mediation; however, it can become harsh at certain times of the day. To cut some light and keep the room cozy, you should install some sheer curtains. These will diffuse the light and keep it serene.

If your room has no natural light, then you need to use light fixtures. Keep the lights semi-bright and use shades and curtains to diffuse them.

If you choose to meditate outside, select a space that does not receive direct sunlight. It should be a shaded corner. If you don't have such a corner, invest in a good umbrella.

10) Good riddance gadgets

One rule that you must follow in your meditation room is getting rid of gadgets. No electronics should be allowed in your meditation room (except music player). Meditation allows you to get away from stress and anxiety for a certain period of time. Gadgets will hinder this process. Avoid having a phone, TV, video games, or any other similar gadget in your meditation room.

Chapter Six: Daily Life and Buddhism

Mindfulness

What is mindfulness?

There is no fixed definition of mindfulness; however, many people define it as a total and nonjudgmental awareness of the current moment. Mindfulness has multiple meanings because it is a state that cannot be expressed in words and can only felt. You need to practice mindfulness at least once to understand what it truly is.

The origin of the concept of mindfulness can be traced back to the Pali word 'sati' or the Sanskrit word 'Smriti.' Both of these words mean 'memory.' But these are literal translations; a precise translation would be 'presence of mind.' Buddha, once upon a time, said, "When we sit, we understand that we are sitting. When we walk, we understand that we are walking. When we consume food, we understand that we are eating." The quote may seem simple, but it points out how Buddha and his followers were always fully present for the act. Mindfulness is so potent that even when a practitioner gets lost in thought, he or she is aware of the fact that he or she has lost himself or herself in thoughts. Mindfulness is being conscious of everything that may arise in the present while concentrating on something. In mindfulness, you observe changes that happen. It is also a motion detector. For instance, a motion detector sits idle if nothing moves or changes, but it gets into the action as soon as something moves.

Similarly, in mindfulness, while concentrating on an object, if nothing moves (i.e., if no sensation, feelings, or thought arise), then the mind stays put. But as soon as one of the above arises, the mind gets into action. Mindfulness is like a dartboard where the point of concentration is the bull's eye. But here, the bull's eye serves as an anchor and not the ultimate goal. In Buddhist meditation, you are not supposed to focus in such a way where everything disappears except your point of concentration.

Mindfulness can be compared to a dream catcher. A dream catcher captures all negative and bad dreams while you are asleep. Similarly, mindfulness captures every thought, sensation, and feeling that arises while 'meditating.' But, here, neither of them caught objects are labeled. You just acknowledge them, and then they are allowed to vanish. While practicing mindfulness, each sensation and feeling that rises comes to your mind automatically. You are supposed to acknowledge it once and then let it go away without thinking about it or judging it.

Mindfulness may seem quite difficult in the beginning. It is human nature to be judgmental. We always try to judge, guess, experience, and understand our thoughts. But in mindfulness, you just acknowledge them. Don't worry if you think that you cannot do this; once you understand mindfulness and start doing it properly, these things will come naturally.

Remember, you are not supposed to reject anything in mindfulness. Mindfulness accepts everything that enters your awareness with open arms. For instance, if you practice mindful walking and certain thoughts arise in your mind, do not reject them just because they interrupt your walking. Observe them, acknowledge them, and then let them go and slowly come back to your original activity. Bring your focus back to your walking. In the beginning, your mind may wander quite a lot, but with habit, time, and practice, you will be able to concentrate and focus without any problems for a long time. Your quality of mindfulness will improve, as well.

Mindfulness has many different 'qualities.' This makes it difficult to define. However, if mindfulness is analyzed with the help of these qualities, then it is possible to understand it as a whole.

Mindfulness is one of the core meditation techniques that has its roots deep-set in Buddhism. It has spread like wildfire all over the world. While this widespread presence of Buddhist practice is welcome, it has been disconnected from its roots. Mindfulness is a great activity, but it can be made much better by accompanying it with the original Buddhist wisdom and teachings. While this disconnection was necessary for the beginning for it to spread, it has been now observed that without the base of Buddhist wisdom, mindfulness has not unlocked its full potential. There are many profound ways to expand your mindfulness. Many simple things can be incorporated in your like to make your daily life more exciting and insightful.

Buddhist mindfulness is based around the 'Four Foundations of Mindfulness.' Most of the modern-day mindfulness practices come from the Satipatthana Sutta. It is believed that Buddha laid down the principles in the 4 Foundations almost 2500 years ago. Almost all of the Buddhist meditation techniques are based on these four principles. Each of the four points provides the practitioner with chances to develop his or her mind, which leads him or her to freedom, independence, peace, serenity, and happiness.

Let us have a quick look at these four foundations one by one.

1. Mindfulness of Physicality

Mindfulness of the physicality, aka Mindfulness of the body, is the first step of Buddhist mindfulness practice. The foundational technique of any mindfulness practice is the mindfulness of breathing. This is often followed by the mindfulness of eating, the mindfulness of chewing, etc. These are some of the examples of mindfulness of positions and movements. Along with physical movements and such, this mindfulness also concerns with our anatomy. This includes various intricacies of our body, such as our internal organs, bodily fluids, etc. While people do not like to talk about these things, Buddha believed that it is necessary to focus and contemplate on them as they allow us to become complete.

A simple meditation that is recommended for this step is as follows:

Sit in meditation posture and slowly concentrate on different parts of your body. This should include your hair, toes, nails, skin, wrinkles, etc. Imagine that you are smiling at each organ.

This mindfulness is essential because it allows us to understand that our body is not a single entity; rather, it is a homogeneous collection of different elements combined together.

Through this step, Buddha wants you to realize the conditioned, selfless, and impermanent nature of reality and things. Once you realize the truth of these, you will be able to let them go and realize the truth.

2. Mindfulness of feelings

This mindfulness is also known as the mindfulness of feelings in feelings. It is easy to understand and follow. It is the mindfulness of pleasurable, painful, and neutral feelings. We feel these feelings through our six sensory organs- the five traditional ones and mind.

This is a crucial stage because it deals with the 3 Poisons of mind according to the Buddhist teachings. These three poisons are hatred, greed, and delusion.

Mindfulness of feelings talks about them in the following manner:

All pleasing feelings lead to attachments, including lust and greed.

All painful feelings lead to problems such as fear and hatred.

All neutral feelings lead to delusion.

Acknowledging feelings will lead to confusion and ultimately suffering. But this does not mean that you should not feel anything at all. You are allowed to experience joy and other emotions, but you should attach yourself to them. Otherwise, these pleasurable moments can transform into suffering as well. Mindfulness can help you avoid these problems properly. It serves as a constant presence that stops us from becoming attached because it provides us with the clarity to understand the truth of reality.

With mindfulness, you feel joy, peace, and other emotions without getting attached to things. A non-attached emotion can lead to the greatest peace that one can experience.

3. Mindfulness of consciousness

Mindfulness of consciousness is also known as the mindfulness of the mind in mind. Buddhist traditions believe that there are 52 mental formations, which include emotions such as fear, joy, anger, excitement, etc. among other things. It should be noted that feelings are just one of the 52 mental formations. These are targeted in the second foundational step, while the rest are focused on in the third stage.

One of the best ways to start mindfulness of consciousness if by focusing on the coming and going of different emotions and states of mind, including fear, joy, anger, etc.

4. Mindfulness of mental objects

This type of mindfulness is also known as the mindfulness of objects of mind in objects of mind. The phrase may sound confusing, but objects of mind are nothing but our ideas, thoughts, and conception.

Perception plays an important role in shaping our reality. Perception can be compared to a television screen. Whatever that is transmitted on the screen is real; however, the image that you see on the screen is not. The image thus is an object of mind. It is not the real thing; rather, it is just a thought or an idea of our mind. This means that we do not experience the object; rather, we experience the image of the object. But this does not mean that the object does not exist. But our experience will always be layered with perception. These perceptions often distort the real experience, either positively or negatively.

The idea of this mindfulness is to allow you to move beyond the world of perception and understand the true experience. For instance, when we love someone, we often love the image of the person that we create in our minds. Once that image is shattered, we start seeing the true nature of the person. It then has a negative (or positive) effect on our attachment. In the practice of mindfulness, this is known as the '5 Hindrances'.

The 5 Hindrances are:

- Lust or sensual longing
- Dullness
- Ill will
- Restlessness and worry
- Doubt

These hindrances hold us back from understanding the truth and thus keep us away from true happiness. These can be defeated with the help of the '7 Factors of Awakening.' They are:

The Seven Factors of Awakening are:

- Mindfulness
- Investigation
- Energy
- Joy
- Tranquility
- Concentration
- Equanimity

Buddha preached that a person needs to cultivate these seven qualities if one wants to achieve true happiness. The first factor of awakening creates a chain effect where each factor is followed almost naturally.

Ultimately, in the practice of mindfulness, it is necessary to remove the 5 Hindrances and invoke the 7 Factors of Awakening.

What's the difference between mindfulness and meditation?

Mindfulness and meditation are both important practices recommended by Buddha. They are often considered to be the same, but they are different. Mindfulness is one of the many forms of meditation, which is why many people often use meditation instead of mindfulness while describing it. This may seem confusing to a beginner. What makes the whole thing even more confusing is that mindfulness is often described in various Pali and Sanskrit terms as well. To avoid confusion, it best to stick with well defined and simple words like mindfulness.

Mindful sitting is also known as sitting meditation. Nowadays, some people also call it mindfulness meditation. Mindful walking is called walking meditation and not mindful walking traditionally. This may increase the confusion of the already confused beginners, especially the people who are learning mindfulness without any guidance.

Meditation consists of many different and broad techniques, but all of them are concerned with the development of the mind. In simpler words, meditation can be defined as a mental technique that is used to make your mind focus on an object (either physical or mental). It is done to develop, grow, and maintain the mind. As said earlier, meditation is a broad concept, and it is possible to define it in many different ways. Many practitioners also say that meditation cannot be defined; it can only be experienced.

Why should you practice Mindfulness?

One of the major causes of our unhappiness, according to Buddha, is mindlessness. The only way to cure this unhappiness is mindfulness; for Buddha, mindfulness was one of the most crucial practices that could change a person's life forever. It was his idea that a person who cannot control his or her destiny is just surviving but not living his life. While there exist many practices that can help you control your mind and destiny, the Buddha believed that mindfulness was the easiest, most approachable, and peaceful method. He believed that mindfulness doesn't just help you to control your destiny, but also your mind and your body. Many Buddhists still believe that a mindless person is like a zombie. Mindfulness can make you alert and bring back you from the land of the zombies.

When you are mindless, you are not in complete control of your mind. The limiting beliefs that are present in everyone try to direct and control your life in such a way that your ego gets protected. Your ego does not care for your wellbeing or happiness; it only cares for itself. This leads to the rise of deep-seated anger and, thus, ultimately suffering.

Along with this, the outside world always tries to pull, push, and control you. Our mind reacts to anything that happens in our life. Mindfulness can allow us to stop or hinder these reactions to save us from suffering. Many times, due to mindlessness, we react in ways that hinder our mental peace and lead to suffering. Mindfulness can help you to prevent this.

Mindfulness can serve an anchor point for you. Almost all of us live our lives in a peculiar manner where we are present physically in one place, but mentally we are in another. We do not live the present; rather, we divide our attention between present, past, and future constantly. What many people do not know is that this leads to a lot of suffering and pain. We continuously want and desire things that we currently do not possess. Along with this, we also spend a lot of time thinking about things that happened in the past and regretting them. We have no control over the past, and thus regretting past things disconnects us from the present. It is as useful as crying over split milk. Living in our own imaginary palaces is often desirable, but it ultimately leads to suffering. It can lead to a variety of problems, including stress, anxiety, pain, suffering, lack of creativity, decreased productivity, etc. It also disconnects us from the present, where we become unable to give time to our loved ones. This again leads to suffering. Instead of enjoying a peaceful and calm life, we continue to live a life with a chaotic, confused, and hurt mind.

In Buddhism, mindlessness is often referred to as 'monkey mind.' All of us have experienced this in our life. Our mind is naughty, and it bounces around from one point to another all the time. It is uncontrollable and jumpy. Only mindfulness can calm our mind as t provides it an anchor point. It is true that your mind may resist the changes in the beginning; however, with time, you will be able to control it and tame it. Once you are able to control your mind, the path to true happiness will open.

Mindfulness and meditation have become so popular in today's world because we are always busy and always connected. It has become extremely easy for everyone to live in a mindless state of being. Mindfulness can help you to get rid of this mindless state without disconnecting you from modern amenities and facilities. This is why Buddhism is growing rapidly in developed and developing nations.

Mindfulness is a versatile practice. Anyone can do it, including adults, children, the elderly, women, men, athletes, students, scientists, soldiers, etc. It is one of the easiest and basic practices of peace, self-healing, and happiness. And all of this has proved by science as well! In the next section, let us have a look at the science behind mindfulness.

Mindfulness and Science

There are a lot of reasons why you should practice mindfulness, and science is just one of them. Science has already proved that meditation is good for our mental health, peace, and serenity, and it can also help in the development of focus and attention. Similarly, mindfulness has many scientific benefits.

Mindfulness has been studied in many scientific studies all around the world. Almost all of these studies have come out with positive results that prove that mindfulness works. Many medical centers, hospitals, schools, and even Silicon Valley has started using it in their courses and curriculum. Everyone is adopting mindfulness because it truly works.

Here is a small list of various benefits of mindfulness that has been proved by different scientific research. All these benefits can help you lead a comfortable and peaceful life. These benefits prove that mindfulness is a necessary practice in today's world. Without mindfulness, our lives become dull, chaotic, problematic, and full of suffering.

Benefits of Mindfulness

As said earlier, there are many benefits of mindfulness. Some of them include:

- Mindful eating can help you lose weight. It can encourage healthy eating habits. It is particularly useful for people who binge eat.

- Mindfulness can help you live longer by enhancing your ability to fight diseases. Yes, mindfulness can boost your immune system and metabolism.

- Mindfulness can decrease various negative emotions, such as pain, stress, tension, etc. While reducing these feelings, it simultaneously enhances and increases positive emotions such as peace, calm, and serenity.

- Mindfulness can help you fight depression. While it can't make it go away completely, it can still help you tackle some of the most severe symptoms.

- Mindfulness can also reduce the effects of PTSD or Post-Traumatic Stress Disorder.

- Mindfulness can increase the density of grey matter present in our brains. Grey matter is essential as it controls and affects functions such as learning, regulation, emotions, memory, etc.

- Mindfulness, as stated above, can help you focus. It can also enhance your attention span. Limited attention span has become a global phenomenon now. Mindfulness can tackle it to make you more attentive.

- Mindfulness is all about living in the present moment. Due to this, many people have reported that they feel more love and compassion. This can also help to improve your relationships.

- Mindfulness can make you more relaxed, at peace, optimistic, satisfied, and accepting of mistakes.

• Mindfulness is great for children and their parents, as well. It can dramatically improve your relationship with your children. Your parenting skills will improve, as well. The children who are taught mindfulness will learn new social skills and become more responsible, compassionate, bold, and friendly.

• Mindfulness can also be a crucial asset for students and teachers. Mindfulness can reduce behavioral problems and aggression in students. It can also enhance their ability to focus. It can also increase their happiness levels. For teachers, mindfulness can reduce negative emotions and can tackle depression as well. It can also lower blood pressure and reduce tension. Many teachers have reported gaining a new sense of empathy, thanks to mindfulness.

Thus it is obvious how mindfulness can change your life for good. If incorporated in your daily life, mindfulness can truly bring in many positive changes.

Practicing Mindfulness

While understanding the theory of mindfulness is important, what is more, important is practicing it. In this section, let us have a look at how you can incorporate mindfulness into your life. Before beginning mindfulness, try to get it under your skin and be comfortable with it. Remember the definition that we saw at the beginning of this article. This will help you remind why and how to do mindfulness practice.

To begin, start examining everything right from the beginning of your day. Try to form a habit of checking on your mind and yourself throughout the day. Randomly ask yourself whether you are present in the present moment or not. Many times it is possible that you may not be present even in the most complex or simplest of things.

We often do not pay attention to what we are doing presently. Binge eating is one of the best examples of this. People often binge eat to either kill time or hide their feelings. For instance, if you are feeling sad and want to avoid it, you start binge eating just to take away attention from the sadness. Soon, the sadness takes over, and you focus on it, but you continue to binge eat as well. This puts in lots of useless calories in your body. People continue to eat even when they are not hungry. Another example of mindless binge eating is while watching television. We get so engrossed in it that we forget that we are eating and mindlessly consume a lot of food. This practice has become a lot more common thanks to a variety of streaming services. These services do not have breaks, and thus you continue to watch and continue to eat mindlessly.

Now that we have covered the beginning of regular mindfulness practice let us move to some simple exercises.

Basic Mindfulness Practice

Sitting

Sitting is one of the most popular ways of meditation. In fact, for many people, meditation and mindfulness equal to sitting. In Buddhism, many different methods, poses, etc. of meditation have been explained. Many people believe that mindfulness is just another name of sitting and meditating. Such people do not understand the purpose of mindfulness or look at it as another gimmick.

You can only create new mental habits when you are mindful. This means if you want to create a new habit quickly, you should be mindful throughout the day. This may seem difficult at first, but with time, you will learn to concentrate and focus without losing your attention.

Walking

Walking is another simple mindfulness exercise. It can be done anywhere and anytime. Many people like walking mindfulness because it allows them to connect with nature while being mindful. But ultimately, it doesn't matter where you walk, etc. Once you start feeling even better, you can walk anywhere and practice walking mindfulness. It is advised to this exercise only when cars and other such things are not present. Walking meditation should not be used as an excuse for jaywalking. But as long as you are taking proper safety precautions and care, you can practice walking mindfulness anywhere. Just see to it that you do not cause other people any trouble.

Following the Breath

This is one of the most versatile forms of mindfulness, as you can do it anytime and anywhere. It is also seen to be an extension of the meditation practice yet; it still posses its own distinct style, which makes it stand out. To do this method, you just need to pay attention to your breathing. You should focus on breath-ins as well as breath-outs. Ensure that your breaths are light, easy, and even. While breathing tries to stay aware of what actions you are doing and where you are.

You should be able to feel the breath going out and coming in. Do not try to control your breathing; just focus on it. It is possible that all this attention will slow down your breathing a bit. Don't worry, just continue to focus on it and do not let your attention go haywire. Breathing is one of the most effective methods of practicing mindfulness. Using breathing as an anchor is easy because it is always present and available.

This method is a brilliant stress buster that allows you to push the pause button for a while. If you are a beginner to the world of mindfulness, then it is necessary to practice it at least 3-4 times a day. This will help you to form a habit of mindfulness. Once the habit is formed, you can change your schedule according to your time, needs, and requirements.

Other Activities

As said earlier, you can practice mindfulness almost anytime, anywhere. Some basic activities where you can practice mindfulness include painting, drawings, brushing your hair, cleaning, doing the dishes, gardening, crocheting, etc. As these activities can be done passively, they are quite easy to do in mindfulness. Practicing mindfulness while talking to people is not impossible, but it is difficult, especially for beginners. With time you will develop enough focus and concentration to do it comfortably.

To practice your mindfulness, just pick up any of the above-mentioned activities and begin. In the beginning, keep the pace of the activities on the slower side. This will make practicing mindfulness easier. Always be 100% committed to that task that you have chosen. Without focus and dedication, mindfulness will prove to be unnecessarily difficult. For instance, if you are washing the dishes, then washing the dishes should become the most crucial thing in the world. You need to be so mindful of the activities that you should feel that the only reason you are doing the dishes is that they should be done. There should be no motive behind the act. If any motive or feeling arise, acknowledge them and let them go. If you continue to do things for motives, then you won't be able to practice mindfulness.

Buddhism in Your Everyday Life

Whenever someone utters the word Buddhism, many people still picture East Asian men dressed in orange, maroon, and yellow robes, sitting down, meditating or chanting mantras peacefully. Some people also think of Buddha beads and serene bell sounds. Some people also think of different planes where suffering does not exist, and only peace and tranquility rules. While all these ideas are different aspects of Buddhism, you should forget that millions of common people follow Buddhism as well. Buddhism is all about spirituality and choosing the middle way, which means not all Buddhists, leave their households, and become monks. It is possible to achieve nirvana while staying and doing your day-to-day life chores as well. In this section, let us have a look at how you can incorporate Buddhism in your day-to-day life or how a Buddhist lives his daily life.

People who research and approach Buddhism are normally haggled, frustrated, and angry at their lives. Such people believe that Buddhism can help them become serene and peaceful. They wish for balance and escape from the chaos that their life has become. There exists a common misconception that to achieve peace in Buddhism, you need to enter another realm. This is false. According to a Buddhist scholar, "A person may walk in space, another might walk on water, yet, the person who walks on earth will always be the greatest.' This explains why Buddhism is often known as the religion of the middle way. The above quote means that you should not detach yourself from your world and discard everything. You cannot lock yourself inside your house just to seek peace. This is not the right way to seek peace. Isolation is not recommended for everyone. It can wreak havoc on not only your mind but your body as well.

Allot Time for Meditation

If you want to be mindful and compassionate, you need to give it some time. Without practicing, you can neither be mindful nor compassionate. Everyone should possess a form of self-awareness so that our minds and bodies can spread out kindness and compassion in the world. Meditation should as natural and as regular as eating. We consume food for physical energy, while meditation can provide you with mental and spiritual energy. If you ever feel that you are too busy to meditate, then you need to check your schedule. A quick practice of mindfulness hardly takes more than a few minutes.

Let us assume that you are a very busy person. Check your schedule if you get any 10-40 minutes break. 10-40 minutes of meditation and mindfulness practice are more than sufficient for extremely busy people. You can also add a small session of about five minutes after having your breakfast. This will keep you fresh throughout the day. Never multitask while meditating. If you do, then the effects of meditation become zero. Avoid thinking about things like your work, bills, family problems, domestic issues, violence, etc. Try to keep your mind as clear as possible. Meditative music can help your mind to become empty quickly. It is true that emptying your mind, in the beginning, will seem difficult; however, with time and practice, you will be able to do it without any problem.

Morning Schedule

Many people have a bad sleep schedule, which means they sleep late and wake up even later, often feeling miserable instead of relaxed and calm. Most of the people wake up in a hurry feeling lethargic. Many times our tardiness creates chaos. If we get stuck at traffic, the chaos and our suffering increase. People get stressed because they do not get any time to do anything properly and peacefully. Ultimately this reflects negatively on our work as well. This creates a sort of phobia in our mind for mornings. The best way to tackle this is by sleeping early and maintaining a proper sleeping schedule.

Mornings are one of the best times to meditate and practice mindfulness. When you wake, take some time out of your busy schedule and practice mindfulness or meditation for some time. This means that you will have to wake early. To wake early, you will have sleep early at night. For this, you may have to forgo some social media time, etc. Social media is one of the most mindless things that you can do as it is addictive and useless. People spend hours together doing nothing or gaining nothing but scrolling down their feed. It is necessary to learn time management. Time management is a skill that can prove beneficial in almost all walks of life.

It is recommended to begin your day with green tea and meditation. Do some breathing exercises and chant mantras or sit down and meditate silently. Meditation opens your mind and makes you more compassionate. These feelings stay with you throughout the day. Even five minutes of early morning meditation can help you defeat stress and pressure of work. Remember, the motto of Buddhism is to spread peace and be at peace as well.

Chanting Mantras

Many schools of Buddhism prescribe different mantras that you can recite or chant to calm yourself. Many theistic schools of Buddhism consider these mantras as prayers dedicated to Bodhisattvas and Buddha's; however, others agree that mantras are atheistic in nature and can be chanted by everyone.

Stress is one of the main culprits behind suffering. When we are stressed, we suffer a kind of breakdown. We grow hateful and start hurting others and ourselves, as well. We often become villainous and start spouting hatred. In such situations, it is necessary to remember why we exist. According to Buddhism, we exist because we want to spread compassion and peace. Even when you feel stressed, try to keep your calm and maintain a positive attitude. Chanting mantras can help you tackle stress. Whenever you feel stressed, start chanting mantras slowly and in a low voice. Always remember the teachings of Buddha and the way that he preached.

Helping Others

Dharma teaches you a lot of things. One of the greatest things that it teaches practitioners are helping and guiding others. You cannot be happy unless other people are happy as well. Everyone needs to work simultaneously to rid this world of pain and suffering. The world is full of misery, and selfishness just adds to it. If we do not help others, we, in turn, will not receive help either. Many Buddhist visit elders, homeless people, jails, soup kitchen, etc. to help and volunteer. You should also help your colleagues, family members, friends, and even the people that you dislike. Treating everyone equally in a fair and justified manner is essential to the teachings of Buddhism.

Remember, Buddhism is not just a religion; rather, it is a philosophy of living your life. Shakyamuni Buddha left the material pleasures of his palace; similarly, we too should surrender our pride and ego. You do not need to leave your day-to-day life, just change it and be mindful about it. Think of yourself as a gardener who plants the seeds of love and compassion. Our world is full of sadness and despair, and the only way to change it by spreading faith, hope, and friendship. Slow down a bit and observe things around; there is no need to rush. Never succumb to the desires of the materialistic world. The society is money-driven, but you should run after it. Spreading love and compassion should be your ultimate goal.

Clearing Your Mind

Meditation is often used to clear and cleanse your mind. Meditation has many different positive aspects. One such aspect is a clear and peaceful mind. Normally, our mind is hyperactive, and it continuously jumps from one point to another. As said earlier, the Buddhists called this monkey mind. People fail to think clearly because our mind continuously bombards us with ideas, thoughts, feelings, and other random things. This often confuses it, causing a lot of problems. This is why learning how to empty your mind is necessary as it can allow you some peace and serenity to think clearly. When the mind is empty, you become less scattered. A sense of self-direction is felt. It allows you to respond to things in a mature and sensible way. You become free of the complex web of thoughts.

For an untrained person, thoughts are automatic and uncontrollable. These people believe that it is impossible to control your mind. This is false, as it has been proven by Buddhism and modern-day psychology that it is possible to teach your mind and influence it. There are many different ways to do this. Most of these methods are related to mindfulness and meditation. Buddha believed that controlling one's mind is essential for enlightenment. Using proper concentration, attention, and focus, you can train your mind and refine it. Let us now have a look at some of the popular methods of training your mind.

Meditation 1: Focus the Mind

For this method, find a calm and secluded place. You should be able to meditate without any distractions for a long time.

Find a comfortable sitting posture and close your eyes.

Focus your attention on any one thing. It can be imaginary or real. Many people use their favorite colors to focus their attention.

Keep your eyes closed and picture the color. If you cannot picture it, try to imagine an object of the same color. For instance, if you are trying to imagine the color green, you can try imagining fresh grass. Once you get the color, stop thinking about any other thing and focus on the color only.

Other feelings, thoughts, and ideas will intrude while you are focusing. Like mindfulness, acknowledge them and then let them fly away gently.

When a sense of calmness comes over you, open your eyes.

This meditation is easy to do and can be done at almost any time of the day. You can also do it wherever you are. In the beginning, you may find it difficult to focus on something for more than a couple of minutes, but with practice and time, you will able to increase the length of your focus and meditation minute by minute. Find your own rhythm and adjust your medication schedule accordingly.

Meditation 2: Beyond Thought

In this method, you are supposed to control your mental chatter. For this, once again, find a serene spot where you can sit or lie down comfortably.

Close your eyes, and once again focus on a color. You can also focus on your breathing or any other object that you want. The object is not important; only the focus is.

If any time an idea or a feeling arises in your mind, acknowledge it gently and then let it subside on its own. Do not pay it any further attention. Return to your meditation at once.

Once again, when another thought arises, acknowledge it, and then disengage yourself from it. Once disengaged, return to your meditation immediately.

Your goal in this form is to stay focused all the time. In the beginning, many thoughts and feelings will arise, but with time your stream of concentration will become more focused. It will become clear, and your mind will become empty. Continue meditating until you feel a sense of inner peace.

Meditation 3: Clearing your Mind

After finishing the above two meditations, you are ready for the third one. You need to practice a lot to focus your mind on something for several minutes without any disturbances. Keep your mind empty of all thoughts.

Try to think of nothing. Your mind should be like to avoid.

In the beginning, do this for thirty seconds only. Slowly increase your time with the help of the above two exercises.

Practicing regularly is essential; try to do it for at least 15 minutes every day.

You may find this step a bit difficult in the beginning, but with time it will seem effortless and natural.

Chapter Seven: Buddhism and Karma

Karma or Kamma in Pali means 'doing' or 'action.' It is an essential concept in many ancient Indian philosophies and teachings. In the Buddhist tradition, karma stands for the action, which is guided by intention. This, in turn, leads to future consequences. These consequences are important as they determine your next birth in the samsara or the cycle of rebirth.

The Buddhist Understanding of Karma

Karma and Karmaphala (the result of karma) are both basic concepts in Buddhism. They are crucial as they explain how our actions keep us chained to the cycle of rebirth. The Buddhist path, which is explained in the Noble Eight-fold Path, can help us escape this cycle.

Rebirth

Rebirth is another common concept that is present in many schools of ancient Indian philosophy. In Buddhist traditions, birth and death occur six times, consequently in successive cycles. These cycles are controlled by avidya, trsna, and dvesa, meaning ignorance, desire, and hatred, respectively. Rebirth is a cyclic entity. This cycle of rebirth is called samsara. It has no beginning, nor does it have an end. You can either continue to be chained to this cycle forever, or you can escape (liberate) using the Buddhist methodology.

Karma and the cycle of rebirth are closely related, as it is karma that decides the fate and facts of the next birth. In the Buddhist tradition, any deed done deliberately through physical, mental, or vocal capacity is karma. This karma, as said earlier, will have some sort of future consequence.

Karmaphala

The results or future consequences of karma are known as karmaphala. Karmaphala literally means the fruits of action. All actions lead to some sort of reaction or results; however, in Buddhism, karmic results are different. Karmic results are the result of the intention of the action along with the moral quality of the action. Karma is more concerned with morality and ethics. It does not concern itself with the relationship between actions and their consequences; rather, it focuses on the moral quality of these actions and their results.

According to the theory of karma, good moral karma will lead to positive rebirths, but negative moral actions will lead to unwholesome rebirths.

Karma is a complex philosophical idea that has been confusing scholars and laymen alike from centuries. For instance, the question of how and why karma leads to rebirth still remains unanswered. Buddhist traditions preach the doctrines of no-self and impermanence, but it also preaches that idea of rebirth. These two ideas are contrasting; however, they have not been reconciled and are still preached simultaneously. There are many reasons behind these contrasting and seemingly confusing aspects of Buddhism, especially in the context of Karma. Buddha was not concerned about philosophical discussions and debates; he was more focused on people becoming enlightened and happy. Often in many Buddhist texts, when a follower would ask a question to Buddha, he would go silent.

In the early days of Buddhism, there exists no explicit theory regarding karma and rebirth. While Buddhism was based on these principles, they were not handled critically. It is also believed that the theory of karma could have arrived in Buddhist schools due to interpolation with other religions and faiths. In early Buddhism, it was believed that desire, ignorance, and cravings lead to rebirth.

In late Buddhism, the idea of karma changed. It was believed that intentional actions are controlled by kleshas or bad emotions, cetna and/or volition, and/or tanha or craving. These intentional actions create tendencies and impressions in our minds. These are known as seeds. These seeds mature and then ripen, which is karmaphala. Thus, to defeat karma, you need to overcome your kleshas. This will break the chain of karma and will stop the cycle of rebirth. You will not be reborn in any of the six realms once you break this cycle. If you are interested in understanding the philosophy of karma in-depth, you can refer to the twelve links of dependent origins. In the twelve links of dependent origins, the whole complex, and theoretical frameworks of karma, rebirth, samsara, and karmaphala are explained properly.

Complex Process

As said earlier, the theory of karma is a complex process. In Buddhism, the theory is not deterministic as such; rather, many circumstantial factors and phenomena are added to it. This is different than the other shamanic religion that developed around the same time, i.e., Jainism. Unlike other Indian religions, the concept of karma is neither rigid nor mechanical in Buddhism. It is fluid, flexible, and dynamic. Buddhists believe that not all present conditions are the result of karma. This is shockingly different than many other interpretations of karma. They believe that there exists no straight relationship between an action and the result it will have. The effect of karma or karmaphala is not determined by the karma or the action itself; rather, it also depends on the nature of the person who committed the action and the situation and circumstances in which the action was done.

Many people often confuse karma with predestination and fate. In Buddhism, karma is a secular concept. Karmaphala is not a form of a judgment given by an almighty God or being. It is considered to be a natural process. Certain actions that we committed in the past are reflected in the experiences that we gain in the present. But how we respond to these experiences is not predestined, yet our response too will have some results in the future. Unjust and bad behavior will lead to unfavorable karmaphala. But unlike other religions and schools of philosophy, you can choose to avoid unjust behavior.

Freedom from Samsāra

The most important factor regarding the doctrine of karma and karmaphala is how to escape it. You are supposed to put all efforts in this direction. Karmaphala is a complex topic. Acintita Sutta, one of the important Buddhist texts, says that the result of karma is one of the four non-understandable subjects. These subjects cannot be comprehended, understood, analyzed, and conceptualized with the help of reason and logic. It serves as a warning to people who try to analyze karma 'backward.' This means that people often tend to think that the unfavorable conditions that they are facing presently are perhaps due to their bad actions in the past. Buddhism avoids such explanations and rather tries to stick to the most important factor of karma, as said above. The ultimate goal of Buddhism is to escape from the cycle of rebirth or the samsara. Focusing on good deeds will let you have a good rebirth, but it will not help you to achieve nirvana.

Within the Pali Suttas

As per the Buddhist tradition, Buddha achieved complete insight into the workings of karma and samsara when he became enlightened. He realized that one could not escape from karma and its result once when the deeds are done, however, many sects and branches of Buddhism believe that it is possible to get rid of bad karma with certain rituals and practices.

According to the Anguttara Nikaya (a Buddhist text), the karmic consequences can be experienced in either this life or the next life. Former will allow you to see the connection between your karma and its results; however, the connection becomes far less obvious and apparent when the results happen in the next life.

According to the Sammyutta Nikaya, there is a difference between present karma and past karma. In the present, a person not only creates new karma, but he or she also experiences the results of his or her past karma.

12 Laws of Karma

The 12 Laws of Karma are not laws per se; rather, they are lessons that help people to live a proper life. These laws are supposed to help you to make the required changes in your life and within yourself. They help you to get rid of bad karma and allow you to collect good karma. If you feel that the world around you is crumbling, it is because you yourself are crumbling. Let us now have a look at the 12 Laws of Karma in brief.

1. The Great Law

The first law is a great law. It is also known as the Law of cause and effect. This law tells us that if we want something, we should embody them.

The message of this law is similar to the Law of Attraction. In simpler words, whatever you give out to the world, the world will give it back to you as well. This means if you want to love, then you cannot give out hatred.

2. The Law of Creation

According to this law, we need to be active participants in our lives if we want something that we desire. Waiting for good things to happen is useless. You need to work for things if you want them.

According to this Law, you need to look at things that are outside to understand what is going on inside you. For instance, if you think that your life is going haywire and that you do not like it, then you should introspect and see whether there is something wrong inside that needs to be changed.

3. The Law of Humility

This law is considered to be quite important in Buddhism. In this law, you are supposed to learn to accept the truth of reality before trying to change it. For instance, if you constantly blame others for causing problems in your life without checking the truth behind your problems, then you will never be able to change it or get rid of the problems either.

4. The Law of Growth

This law says that you ultimately have control over yourself only, and if you want to see a change in the world, you need to change yourself first. Focusing on your development instead of trying to change or control others will ultimately help you achieve the desired results.

5. The Law of Responsibility

It is necessary to remember that you are the source of what happens throughout your life. What happens around you is, in a way, a mirror to what is happening inside you. This means you are responsible for all the nastiness, the hatred, or the pleasantness that is present around you.

6. The Law of Connection

The Law of Connection can help people to remove bad karma from their life. In this law, the connection between your past, present, and future is emphasized. It teaches how you can control your present to manipulate your future and also remove the bad energy from the past.

7. The Law of Focus

This law says that focus and attention are essential if you want to achieve something in your life. It is always better to follow a single thought instead of spreading yourself too thin. If you have multiple goals, set your priorities straight and work on them one by one.

8. The Law of Giving and Hospitality

This law talks about the connection present between practice and belief. It believes that the lessons that we learn in our life are often tested.

9. The Law of Here and Now

Buddhism is all about accepting the truth of your reality. You are supposed to live in the present, and if you cling too hard to your past, you will not be able to move forward. This law believes that you should always live in the present while caring for the future and the past, as well.

10. The Law of Change

This law addresses the fact that the universe only gives you things that you desire for. According to this law, history will continue to repeat itself in a loop because you have failed to address something fundamental. If you see that things have changed suddenly around you, then it is because you addressed this fundamental issue and are now moving towards growth.

11. The Law of Patience and Reward

This law says that to achieve great success, you need to be persistent, patient, and dedicated. You cannot achieve something without any effort. Immediate results are rare; you need to work hard if you want to be successful.

12. The Law of Significance and Inspiration

According to this law, whatever you do contributes to your life and the world around you. Even if you do the littlest positive thing, it will be reflected back towards you. You may sometimes feel insignificant in this gigantic world, but you should remember that you matter. Your absence would change the universe significantly.

Thus, this was an in-depth chapter about various beneficial practices and aspects of Buddhism. Karma and karmaphala are very important and at the same time, very confusing aspects of Buddhism. These concepts often confuse esteemed scholars, as well. If you ever feel confused while practicing Buddhism or reading this book, just come back to this chapter and revise it.

Chapter Eight: Buddhism for Kids

Buddha preached thousands of sermons and ideas, out of which only a few were directed towards children specifically. There are only 3-5 sermons that target children specifically. Buddha preached thousands of sermons related to a multitude of subjects. Children have always been an integral part of all cultures, so it is quite a shock why Buddha did not preach more sermons for the children. According to some people, Buddha did not preach to children because he believed that to follow his path, it was necessary to possess a sound, adult, and mature mind. Buddhism is about commitment, and Buddha believed that the children would not be able to commit to his ideas, code of conduct, and rules. Another theory indicates that perhaps centuries ago, children were firmly controlled by the family, and thus the family was supposed to imbibe the teachings of Buddha in them. This is how education worked in ancient Indian society anyway. Until a specific age, children were taught valuable lessons by their adults, and after becoming slightly mature, they were sent off to the household of a teacher. Some people also believe that thanks to the innocence and compassionate nature of the children, Buddha did not find it necessary to teach them Dharma as they already followed it anyway.

Buddha was a father himself. Prince Siddhartha had a son named Rahula. Rahula is Pali for 'shackle.' When prince Siddhartha realized the truth of existence, he left and abandoned all of his family and materialistic pleasure to search for the truth of reality. Fathers who abandon their children have been a typical trope in the literature of almost all cultures. Normally, these fathers are portrayed in a negative light. However, in the case of Buddha, this abandoning is positive. Instead of calling it abandonment, many people prefer to refer to it as renunciation. Buddha renounced his royal duties, material pleasures, his family, and his son because he wanted to seek unconditional happiness. He knew that while seeking this happiness, the above things would act as shackles. He also knew that if he were ever to succeed in understanding the truth of reality, he would be able to preach it to his family as well.

Rahula was seven years old when he was accepted as a disciple of his father. He soon began his training to become a monk. The discourse that is associated with Rahula is known as Rahula Sutta. In this discourse, Buddha instructed his son and taught him many things about the Dharma. Buddha stressed the essence of being truthful and how crucial it is for enlightenment. He told Rahula that if he ever wanted to find the truth, he should be truthful to himself. Later, Buddha explained our actions are mirrored by the world. This means that if we want to love from the world, then we need to give the world love. He then taught his son to analyze actions and ideas before acting upon them. If the idea would lead to a negative or harmful action, then he asked him to abstain from it. If it would lead to a positive outcome, then Rahula was allowed to continue with the idea. Once you are done with the action, you should again ask yourself whether the action that you did had a positive effect or negative effect. If it brought positive effect, then great, but if it didn't, and the effect turned out to be negative, then talk about it with someone and choose wisely next time.

Buddha understood the importance of learning from your mistakes and thus taught the same to his son. He taught Rahula how important it was to take responsibility for his own actions. He also preached to him the importance of compassion and how one can cultivate it. But along with these things, Buddha also taught Rahula about how causality works and the cycle of karma. He taught how things have future reactions, along with immediate reactions. Buddha also taught Rahula the basics of the Four Noble Truths. He told him how suffering is caused due to present and past actions and how we can avoid them and ultimately achieve complete freedom from the cycle of karma.

Buddha believed that teaching children spiritual practice could help them immensely. In the era of Buddha, the children were already surrounded by an atmosphere of spirituality and instructions. They had very few distractions. The cultural practices were different, as well. Due to the combination of all these factors, instructing children and asking them to practice meditation and mindfulness was simple. The times have changed now, and getting children to follow these practices has become difficult. Raising kids as Buddhists in today's time is difficult because of the number of distractions and the changed cultural practices as well. To inculcate Buddhist values in children, parents need to form a base first. Sometimes it will be necessary for you to start from scratch. Such parents can utilize the Rahula Sutta and many other teachings of Buddha. These will make their job comparatively easier. If the parents have been practicing Buddhism for a long time, then getting children interested in it will not be a difficult task. Children love to imitate their elders; if you yourself practice Buddhism regularly, children too will start following you.

Another method of getting children interested in Buddhism is through the use of cartoons, comics, animations, stories, movies, etc. You can try to make your lessons interesting, fun, and interactive for the children. Many East Asian nations have produced significant material on Buddhism for children. But remember, just preaching will not help you; you need to make children understand how important and useful the lessons of

Buddhism can be. You should make them understand how meditation, compassion, mindfulness, love, and other teachings of Buddhism can help them in day-to-day life. You can force a child to learn something, but you can never force him or her to love something.

H. Stephen Glenn, one of the most celebrated educators and parenting guides who wrote books, including the best seller Raising Self-Reliant Children in a Self-Indulgent World many times, said how Western parents are pioneers. But he believed that these parents do not understand the benefits of being a pioneer.

Parents all over the world learn the skills of parenting from their parents, elders, family members, neighbors, etc. We copy the skills and methods of others. Due to this, all of us have similar parenting skills and methodology. Another reason why these skills are similar is that all of us live in the same community. The community as a whole shares values, emotions, and goals. This is was highly common in the ancient, medieval, and to some extent, pre-world war world. But after the World Wars, cultural traditions changed. Many different factors changed how we lived, interacted with each other, etc. In a way, cultural harmony and the feeling of the community changed forever. The Depression, industrial boom, rapid rise of capitalism, continuous wars, cold war, the explosion of technology, and money changed our world forever. The role and methodology of parenting changed rapidly and drastically, as well. What was once a cumulative work, a task for the community, now became a solitary duty. Parents lost the support of their elders, neighbors, parents, experts, etc. and parenting became a struggle for the couple. The world continues to change, and instead of parenting becoming easier, it continues to become more and more difficult. This is why many parents focus on experimenting and trying new things for their children.

This pioneering aspect often leads to positive results.

The situation of parents and Buddhists in the modern world is similar. Modern Buddhists are trying to steer children away from the materialistic world as it causes suffering. Teaching Dhamma to children may be difficult, but with ample practice, children will surely grow to love it.

Buddhism and How to Raise Children

Parents all around the world are always confused and worried about whether they are raising their children right or not. Parenting is one of the most difficult tasks in the world because if you mess up, you end up ruining the life of a whole family. While many people have adopted different modern ways to raise their kids, some parents believe that going back to the ancients can help them become better parents. These parents look for ancient methods, principles, techniques, and skills that can help them improve. Many ancient teachers, including Buddha, have influenced people for generations and have helped them find the truth of reality as well. Buddha's teachings are universal and can be applied anywhere, anytime, and do anything as well. However, as said earlier, Buddha did not provide us with any specific sermons, advice, or techniques for parenting and raising children. As said earlier, there are many reasons why Buddha did not teach his followers how to raise children. But, parents should not be worried, because as said above, Buddha's teachings are universal, and thus you can use these teachings to improve your parenting skills. Let us have a look at some examples.

1) Authenticity

Buddha believed that preaching could only reach a certain audience. To reach out to more people, you need to act and show them how things can be changed. Children do not like listening to sermons. It is difficult to get a young child to focus just on words. Children, especially young ones, love to imitate. They copy our ways. Many children pick up the way their parents walk, talk, dress, and act in public. Children are naturally curious, and they love to question and check things. They are also good observers. So, for instance, if you preach the teachings of Buddha, such as, love, compassion, devotion, wisdom, etc. but act the opposite, children we see through you and will never learn or respect you. You cannot preach wisdom and act neurotically. Similarly, you cannot expect your children to be compassionate if you act selfish and self-centered around them. Your spiritual practice will not work on your children if you do not practice what you preach.

2) Personal Practice

To teach someone, you first need to learn. If you want to raise a smart, emotional, and social child, you need to set an example for him or her. You can set an example with your own practice. Mindfulness practice is a great way to develop emotional intelligence. In mindfulness practice, we are able to empty our minds so that we can be calm and peaceful. As mentioned in the previous chapters, while doing a mindfulness practice, if a thought occurs in your mind, acknowledge it and let it disappear on its own. Do not deal with it or engage with it. Mindfulness practice teaches you to be non-judgmental, and it opens your mind. It helps us connect with our fears and hopes. This practice is crucial in households with young children. It will allow you to share your life with them with ease.

3) Surrender

Parents need to learn how to surrender if they ever want to become good parents. You should be able to surrender everything for your child. Often you will be forced to surrender things like mental peace, tranquility, sleep, and many other crucial things. But as said earlier, a parent cannot be selfish. Children are curious, young, and immature; it is necessary to let them act like children. While discipline is important, you should never overdo it. If you cannot surrender yourself, then a sort of tug of war is formed between you and your children, which leads to constant struggle, pain, and suffering on both sides. Your children will try to compete with you and will try to break your ego as well. Children are human beings with emotions and feelings. As their parents, your duty is to nurture them and not manage them. If you want to raise good and successful children, you need to learn how to sacrifice. You need to forgo your desires and wants and shift the energy towards parenting instead.

4) Let Go

As said earlier, mindfulness is one of the best ways to connect with children. Children who practice mindfulness regularly learn a lot of things about themselves. They understand their dreams, their reality, their capacity, and their wellbeing as well. As parents, we often have dreams about the future of our children. Many times these dreams are actually our unfulfilled dreams that we want them to fulfill. But these are our dreams, and it is possible that the children may have different ideas and plans. With the help of mindfulness, you can create a space where everything is accepted with love and kindness. Children can express their dreams in this space without any fear or guilt. Letting go while parenting is essential. We cannot control the fates of others, including our children. They should be free to live their lives however they want.

5) The Mundane is Sacred

Children live in the present and are often engrossed at the moment. They do not understand or even know the doctrines, experiences, and facts of Buddhism. They also are not aware of the politics, social conditions, economics, etc. around them. For children, especially younger, their whole experience and life revolves around their house. This is why it is crucial to act early if you want to influence your children. Once your children become mature enough to leave the house on their own, your chances of influencing them decrease rapidly. Mindfulness can help you influence your children effectively. It can help you teach your children how to observe and appreciate things. It can really fertilize the young and still-growing minds of the children. The more you practice it, the better your children will become.

The principles of Buddhism can really bring a great difference in the lives of parents, their children, and their family. If your children are too young, it is recommended to start slowly, or else these practices may overwhelm them.

Conclusion

Buddhism is one of the most ancient schools of philosophy. It is a complex family of religions with many different beliefs, theories, and ideas. Yet, what makes it so popular even now is scientific and rational it is. No other religion in this world is as logical and rational as Buddhism.

We live in a world full of desire. As said earlier, desire is the root cause of suffering, so in a way, we live in a world of pain and suffering. Everyone has problems, and everyone wants to live a life full of peace and tranquility. But due to the constraints of modern life and the ever-growing competition, these things have become virtually impossible. Stress has become such an integral part of our lives that people complain of feeling stressed in dreams as well. Our beautiful dreamlike lives have turned into never-ending nightmares.

Buddhism is one of the best ways to tackle stress and anxiety. A complex collection of various sects and practices, Buddhism is highly adaptive and flexible. You can incorporate it into your daily life without disturbing your schedule. It can also be included in your religious practices thanks to its secular nature. As said earlier, Buddhism is a complex group of practices and beliefs, which is why it can prove to be difficult to understand. Many people find it confusing and befuddling. This book can help you get rid of all these confusions. I am sure that all your queries regarding Buddhism must have been answered in this book. This book is a simple but in-depth guide to Buddhism. It explains the principles of Buddhism in a lucid, simple, concise, yet clear manner.

One of the main features of Buddhism is its rational nature. It makes you introspect to understand that all your problems are created by you. To find true happiness, you need to understand this and solve these problems one by one. You can neither find the problems nor the solutions outside. This book can help you find solutions to these problems. It contains various codes of practice according to the Buddhist principle that can help you live an ideal and peaceful life.

This book has been divided into eight well-researched and in-depth chapters. All these chapters contain information derived, collected, and simplified from various resources. Chapters covering basic information regarding Buddhism, such as the life and death of Buddha, the rise of Buddhism, the various beliefs and practices of Buddhism, are covered in the beginning. As there are many different kinds of Buddhism currently being practiced in the world, a novice may get confused; for this purpose, a special chapter has been dedicated to various schools of Buddhism. Buddhism contains various special codes and teachings- these include the Four Noble Truths, the Three Jewels, The Eightfold Path, etc. all of these have been covered in detail in this book. These ideas are essential for any Buddhists, and thus ample attention has been given to them. A special section has been dedicated to the place and importance of Buddhism in the modern world.

Many people are confused regarding Yoga and Buddhism. A lot of people believe that these two are the same thing. A special section has been devoted to this confusion. Buddhism is all about karma, rebirth, and escaping the cycle of rebirth as these concepts can be quite confusing, especially for beginners. For this, these concepts have been covered in detail.

Meditation and mindfulness are two essential practices of Buddhism. Both of these have become so popular that they have entered popular culture in the West as well. Mindfulness has taken the world by storm. Everyone is talking about it and how it has changed their life for good. In this book, mindfulness and many different forms of meditation are covered extensively. A special section has been dedicated to the relationship between mindfulness and Buddhism and how, by incorporating Buddhist wisdom in mindfulness, can you make it more effective and potent.

A small chapter has been dedicated to children, their parents, and Buddhism. It will prove to be an asset for parents who are planning or trying to raise their children as Buddhists.

The promises that were made in the introduction have been fulfilled. This book not only provides you the theoretical aspects of Buddhism but also guides you through the practical aspects, including meditation and mindfulness. Mindfulness truly can provide you the inner peace that you have desired desperately. Mindfulness, along with Buddhism, can help you overcome stress and anxiety, as explained in the book. Truly it can change your life for good.

Buddhism is truly a life-changing experience, but if you are still confused about whether you should incorporate it in your life for not, then the best way to test the waters is by trying mindfulness and meditation. These two are perfectly secular Buddhist practices that can be practiced by followers of any religion. Follow these practices with complete dedication and efforts. I am sure that you will soon start noticing positive changes in your life.

Ultimately, it should be understood that Buddhism is like a never-ending sea of knowledge. It is impossible to cover it in a few chapters, or even a few books. Let this book be your guide to the path of Buddhism. Use this book as a starting point to enter the peaceful world of Buddhism.

In conclusion, let us once again take refuge in the Three Jewels of Buddhism.

Buddham Sharanam Gacchami

Dhammam Sharanam Gacchami

Sangham Sharanam Gacchami

References

https://tricycle.org/beginners/buddhism/what-do-buddhists-believe-happens-after-death/

https://tricycle.org/beginners/buddhism/what-happened-after-the-buddha-died/

http://factsanddetails.com/world/cat55/sub355/item1336.html

https://archive.artsmia.org/art-of-asia/buddhism/buddhism-origins.cfm

https://www.lamayeshe.com/article/what-mind

https://www.pbs.org/edens/thailand/buddhism.htm

https://tricycle.org/magazine/four-noble-truths/

https://www.pursuit-of-happiness.org/history-of-happiness/buddha/

Müller, M., & Maguire, J. (2002). Dhammapada: Annotated & Explained. Woodstock, VT: SkyLight Paths Publishing. (Translation by Max Müller, annotations and revisions by Jack Maguire.)

Smith, H. (1991). The World's Religions. New York, NY: HarperCollins, Inc.

https://studybuddhism.com/en/advanced-studies/history-culture/buddhism-in-modern-times/the-appeal-of-buddhism-in-the-modern-world

https://www.quora.com/What-is-the-concept-of-mind-in-Buddhism

https://tricycle.org/magazine/noble-eightfold-path/

https://www.beliefnet.com/faiths/buddhism/2005/04/the-three-jewels-of-buddhism.aspx

https://en.wikipedia.org/wiki/Five_preceptszhttps://www.lionsroar.com/the-middle-way-of-stress-september-2012/

https://www.lionsroar.com/category/how-to/

https://mindworks.org/blog/buddhist-meditation-techniques-practices/

https://www.quora.com/What-is-the-relationship-between-yoga-and-buddhism

https://studybuddhism.com/en/advanced-studies/history-culture/interreligious-dialogue/combining-yoga-with-buddhist-practice

https://freshome.com/2014/12/23/10-ways-to-create-your-own-meditation-room/

https://www.depressionalliance.org/12-laws-of-karma/

http://www.thelawofattraction.com/12-laws-karma/

https://en.wikipedia.org/wiki/Karma_in_Buddhism

https://tricycle.org/magazine/introduction-teaching-your-children-buddhist-values/

https://www.lionsroar.com/ask-the-teachers-23/

http://meditation.radiantdolphinpress.com/clearmind.htm

https://matt-valentine-nr5w.squarespace.com/blog/what-is-mindfulness-guide

https://buddhaimonia.com/blog/buddha-guide-to-mindfulness-practice

https://www.tibetanbuddhismconference.com/buddhism-in-your-everyday-life/

https://blog.sivanaspirit.com/bd-sc-buddhas-advice-raising-children/

Gratitude, Joy, Inspiration & Love,

Healing, motivation, inspiration, challenge and guidance straight to your inbox every week....

FIND OUT MORE

www.ingramcontent.com/pod-product-compliance
Lightning Source LLC
Chambersburg PA
CBHW032359100526
44587CB00010BA/515